Tolkien and The Silmarillion

J. R. R. Tolkien's *The Silmarillion* has been one of
the most eagerly awaited books of this century. It
tells the story of Middle Earth before the events of
The Lord of the Rings.

Clyde Kilby spent a summer working with Tolkien on
the manuscript of *The Silmarillion*. In this book he
describes that time. He builds up a fascinating
portrait of Professor Tolkien, his work as a Christian
writer, and his friendship with C. S. Lewis, Charles
Williams and the rest of 'The Inklings'.

Clyde Kilby is Curator of the Wade Collection of
materials associated with Tolkien and Lewis. His
previous books include *The Christian World of C. S.
Lewis* and, with Douglas Gilbert, *C. S. Lewis:
Images of His World*.

To Betty and Gene,
Becky and Pete,
Jeannette and Stan

An Aslan Book

TOLKIEN AND THE SILMARILLION

Clyde Kilby

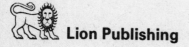 **Lion Publishing**

LION PUBLISHING
121 High Street, Berkhamsted, Herts
Copyright © 1976 Harold Shaw Publishers, USA

First UK edition 1977

ISBN 0 85648 078 9

Printed in Great Britain by
J. W. Arrowsmith Ltd., Bristol BS3 2NT

Contents

Preface

The plan for this little book could hardly be simpler. It originated in a request from the editor of Kodon, *the literary magazine of Wheaton College, for an article on J. R. R. Tolkien. In the several months intervening between the request and my actual writing of the article we were all shocked and grieved over the news of Professor Tolkien's death on September 2, 1973. This sad event added to my feeling that perhaps a record of my acquaintance with him, and particularly my experience as reader of* The Silmarillion, *might be significant.*

This book makes no claim to biography. That must be left to someone far better acquainted with Tolkien than I, perhaps one of his own family. Even there I have the feeling that it will not be a simple matter. Tolkien's son Michael reports being asked innumerable times what kind of person his father was and what took place inside the walls where his great mythological world was engendered and grew up. The son confesses that he finds such questions difficult, if not actually impossible, to answer clearly and definitely.

I felt that Tolkien was like an iceberg, something to be reckoned with above water in both its brilliance and mass and yet with much more below the surface. In his presence one was aware of a single totality but equally aware at various levels of a kind of consistent inconsistency that was both native—perhaps his genius—and developed, almost deliberate, even enjoyed. The word, if there were one, might be "contrasistency." If my account of him is sketchy and in itself inconsistent, it has the virtue of reflecting my real impression of the man.

Neither is this intended to be a comprehensive introduction to Tolkien. That also would be a large and difficult task. Though I have written as succinctly and honestly as I know how, this book is little more than a straightforward record of my experience of personal contact with him during the assigned task of reading The Silmarillion.

I extend to Professor Christopher Tolkien, literary executor of his father's papers, the assurance of my sincerest interest in his efforts to bring The Silmarillion *to publication. I know that thousands of others feel as I do and will welcome the appearance of the story of the First Age of Middle-earth. To my readers I can give the assurance of Professor Tolkien's earnest labors to bring together all the parts of* The Silmarillion *at the earliest time consistent with the painstaking accuracy he is seeking.*

My thanks are due the Mythopoeic Society for the use, with changes and corrections, of an address on "Tolkien, Lewis and Williams" which I gave at its annual meeting in Claremont, California, and is published in the Mythcon I Proceedings *for 1971, also for a brief article I wrote at the time of Tolkien's death. I am also grateful to Kodon at Wheaton College for permission to use the account of my first meeting with Tolkien. Here also, however, I have made revisions.*

For assistance I am indebted to my colleagues, Professors Erwin Rudolph and Arthur Rupprecht, to Miss Barbara Griffin, Librarian of the Marion E. Wade Collection at Wheaton College, to Mr. Paul Snezek, Miss Ivy Olson and Miss Jorena Ryken, as well as students Kristi Wheeler and Linda Detambel.

I am grateful to Professor George Sayer for his encouragement in connection with the completion of this manuscript, to Professor Colin Hardie of Oxford and Professor David Jeffrey of Victoria University, and particularly to Professor Christopher Tolkien of Oxford, who was kind enough to look over the manuscript, also to Mr. and Mrs. Glen GoodKnight who read the whole manuscript and made suggestions for improvements. Let it be said, however, that I do not in any wise make these responsible for my own shortcomings.

I express thanks to all those quoted, especially to the estates of J. R. R. Tolkien and C. S. Lewis for permission to use the works of these writers, including some unpublished letters.

My very greatest feeling of gratitude goes to Wheaton College for allowing me two winter quarters freedom for this and

---

other writing, to the Marion E. Wade Collection at Wheaton with its excellent holdings, and to Dr. and Mrs. Gene Wheeler of Dallas, Texas, who graciously provided a hidden retreat in the hills of north Texas surrounded by cows, horses, geese, ducks, swans and meadowlarks and containing a fireplace of almost unequalled proportions.

And for valuable assistance in various ways I thank Martha.

J. R. R. Tolkien

I

First
Meeting

I first met J. R. R. Tolkien late on the afternoon of September 1, 1964. His fame was then rapidly on the rise and he had been forced to escape his public whenever he could. Visitors were more or less constantly at his door and his telephone busy. Phone callers from the United States sometimes forgot the time differential and would get him out of bed at two or three o'clock in the morning. He was paying the price of his sudden emergence from the relative obscurity of a professional scholar to the glare of publicity accorded to any internationally known writer.

Knowing the reported difficulty of getting inside his house, I asked for help from his personal physician, Dr. Robert E. Havard, who then lived at 28 Sandfield Road, not far from the Tolkien home. After an exciting hour of conversation over tea in Dr. Havard's garden, I inquired how I might contrive to get into Tolkien's presence. What I hoped was that Dr. Havard would telephone and introduce me. Instead he said, "Just go down there and ring the door-bell. He isn't doing anything."

With great hopes and some fears I walked to 76 Sanfield Road, opened the gate, nervously approached his door and rang the bell. I waited what seemed to me a very long time and was on the point of a reluctant departure when the door opened and there stood the man himself.

Tolkien matter-of-factly invited me inside but added that in only a few minutes he had to go out. We went into his downstairs office, remodeled from a one-car garage. Possessing no automobile, he was then using taxis for errands to Oxford, two miles away, and elsewhere. This little office was pretty well filled up with a desk, a couple of chairs, and bookcases along the walls.

After his sober greeting at the door, I found him immediately friendly as we sat down. Tolkien was a most genial man with a steady twinkle in his eyes and a great curiosity—the sort of person one instinctively likes. The main reason which was forcing him to shut out visitors was not his antipathy to them but rather the knowledge that his natural friendliness and love of talking with almost anybody who happened along would seduce him into spending time with visitors while his work languished.

I briefly explained who I was and told him that, like thousands of others, I had come to love his great story and regard it as something of a classic. He laughed at the idea of being a classical author while still alive, but I think he was pleased. He then became a bit apologetic and explained that people sometimes regarded him as a man living in a dream world. This was wholly untrue, he insisted, and described himself as a busy philologist and an ordinary citizen interested in everyday things like anybody else. As an illustration of his practicality he told me of his keen regret that salaries were raised at his college at Oxford the very day after his retirement. He had begun at Oxford as Rawlinson and Bosworth Professor of Anglo-Saxon and later became Professor of English Language and Literature at Merton College, remaining there until his retirement in 1959.

Tolkien was happily aware of the increasing popularity of his books in the United States and elsewhere and hopeful that sales would continue to increase.

He talked of *The Silmarillion*, commenting that his main trouble with it was the lack of a commanding theme to bring the parts together. He was much aware that he needed to complete the story and spoke of his hope to publish it by 1966. He recounted some of the plot, especially its beginning. At that time I had no idea I should later read the story in manuscript.

He told me, surprisingly, that he and his good friend C. S. Lewis had long before agreed to do narratives dealing with space and time. Lewis wrote *Out of the Silent Planet* and *Perelandra* and thus fulfilled his part of the plan to write on space, but Tolkien said he had never embarked on a story about time.

He and Lewis had begun their careers at Oxford University in the year 1925 and were close friends. Later they were both prominent in the "Inklings", where members read their manuscripts to each other for pleasure and the benefit of criticism. The two men had often taken walks together. Only once had Tolkien been with Lewis on one of the long walking holidays Lewis enjoyed so much. They had hiked in the neighborhood of Minehead in the southwest of England. Tolkien concluded that twenty-five miles a day over rough country with a heavy pack on his shoulders was more than he preferred, so he had confined himself thereafter to shorter jaunts nearer Oxford with his friend.

To my surprise, at the end of our brief visit, Tolkien warmly invited me back for the morning of September 4, the day before I was to fly home to the U.S. At that time Mrs. Tolkien greeted me at the door and showed me upstairs to her husband's main office, a room crowded with a large desk, a rotating bookcase, wall bookcases, and a cot. I was received like a longtime friend.

I was by no means unhappy to find him doing nearly all

the talking. It was a pleasure to listen as he went easily from one topic to another. Tolkien, himself a Catholic, told anti-Catholic anecdotes with a glow of humor and an utter lack of antagonism. One story was of Lewis's Anglican childhood in North Ireland where he had been told that the wiggletails in a well at his home were wee Popes. Such stories, I later found, did not mean that Tolkien had a casual view of his religion.

While he talked he stood up and walked about or else sat on his cot. Like C. S. Lewis, when I visited him some years earlier, Tolkien continually fiddled with his pipe but actually smoked little. As his talk grew in enthusiasm, he would sometimes come very close to me and put his face almost against mine, as though to make sure the point of some remark was completely understood. One had the feeling that he had thought considerably about whatever opinion he was expressing and simply wanted to state it accurately. While he could not go long without a brightening of his eyes over some anecdote that might tumble out, he could also be very sharp in his antagonism to anything he thought awry in the community or the world. Once he spoke of a certain well-known person in Oxford as "one of God's congenital idiots."

He told me that he was fourteen years writing *The Lord of the Rings*, also that he had typed all of it himself, with many changes, by the three-fingers method, in the very room we were in. I asked him how *The Hobbit* was related to *The Lord of the Rings* and whether he had gotten the idea of the latter while doing the former. He promptly insisted this was not the case. The stories originated, he said, in orbits of their own and neither was necessarily the consequence of the other. He admitted that the manuscript of *The Lord of the Rings* was sold through his agent to Marquette University because he needed money, owing to his having been "retired on a pittance." (Later I learned from Marquette that the manuscripts made a stack seven feet high.)

I asked how he went about inventing the hundreds of names of characters and places, and he said he did it by a "mathematical" system. He meant, I think, that his inventions, including his Elvish languages, arose not simply out of imagination but from his professional knowledge of the origin and growth of languages themselves and particularly from his experience in the worlds of Nordic, Teutonic and Celtic mythology. He was also aware of an even deeper meaning and origin for his fiction. He said that a Member of Parliament had stood in the room we were in and declared, "*You* did not write *The Lord of the Rings*," meaning that it had been given him from God. It was clear that he favored this remark.

I asked why he did not come to America. He told me that long before our visit Marquette University had invited him to accept an honorary degree, but after he had bought steamship tickets an illness of his wife prevented their departure.

As I prepared to leave, he spoke of getting a letter from a man in London whose name was Sam Gamgee. I asked him what reply he had made and he said he had written that what he really dreaded was getting a communication from S. Gollum. He gave me an autographed copy of *Tree and Leaf* and was about to do the same with another book to which he had contributed but found that he had only one copy of it.

II

Summer
With Tolkien

When I left Tolkien's home in 1964 I had no idea of ever returning. We carried on a little correspondence. One item of it concerned the possible publication of a manuscript of his called *Mr. Bliss*, a children's story written and illustrated by him somewhat in the Beatrix Potter style. He concluded that, in his words, this story would not "enhance" his reputation and it still remains among various other writings yet to be published.

Another topic of correspondence concerned a plan developed late in 1964 to establish at Wheaton College a collection, or set of collections, including his works and those of C. S. Lewis, Charles Williams, Dorothy Sayers, G. K. Chesterton, George MacDonald and Owen Barfield. I wrote him that we planned to bring together "everything you have written and everything written about you, both in books and periodicals." Of course we also desired manuscripts. He told me that with his major manuscript already sold he felt his others should be left to his heirs. Later on he did offer us, after its publication, the manuscript of *Smith of Wootton Major*, and we made the best price we could, but it was less than he anticipated.

Another item of correspondence had to do with my sending him copies of feature articles which from time to time came to my attention. I eventually found that such things so displeased him it was just as well not to send them at all. Reporters, he assured me, always got things wrong. Actually Tolkien was not the sort of person, if indeed anyone is, who could be captured in the oversimplification of the feature article. This was especially true of articles which emphasized him as a cult-figure and something more or less than human. This attitude may have been why Tolkien managed so remarkably to keep the events of his actual life hidden from the public. Of some of the features published about him, he remarked that too many people thought him "a gargoyle to be gaped at."

Then in the latter part of 1965 I wrote him that, like many others, I was eager to see *The Silmarillion* published and would therefore come to Oxford during the summer of 1966, if he wished, to assist him with his correspondence or in any other manner that might facilitate the publication of his story of the First Age of Middle-earth. On Christmas Eve I found the following letter in my mail:

I am very sorry that your letter written on November 19th has not yet been answered. I was deeply touched by it, indeed overwhelmed by your generosity in offering to sacrifice your precious time (and holiday) in helping me. But when your letter came to me I was rather burdened and distracted. My wife's health for more than a month has given me much anxiety (and necessitated my going twice to the Southwest in the interim with much loss of time, but became worse with the sudden early onset of winter). A competent part-time secretary, after giving me much assistance with Ballantine business, departed. And I was suddenly presented with the necessity of revising, and correcting the proofs of, *The Hobbit* for new editions. Each day I thought it would be done, but I only got off the last material a few days ago. However, the mere burden of correspondence has been eased. Unexpectedly a competent secretary appeared, after 11 years assisting David Cecil. She is brisk and orderly, but has no knowledge of my work. So that I am not in such straits as to allow you to spend your valuable time on mere correspondence. . . .

I have never had much confidence in my own work, and even now when I am assured (still much to my grateful surprise) that it has value for other people, I feel diffident, reluctant as it were, to expose my world of imagination to possibly contemptuous eyes and ears. But for the encouragement of C. S. Lewis I do not think that I should ever have completed or offered for publication *The Lord of the Rings. The Silmarillion* is quite different, and if good at all, good in quite another way, and I do not really know what to make of it. It began in hospital and sick-leave (1916-1917) and has been with me ever since, and is now in a confused state, having been altered, enlarged, and worked out, at intervals between then and now. If I had the assistance of a scholar at once sympathetic and yet critical, such as yourself, I feel I might make some of it publishable. It needs the actual *presence* of a friend and adviser at one's side, which is just what you offer. As far as I can see, I shall be free soon to return to it, and June, July and August are available. (As at present advised I am booked to take my wife on a cruise in the Mediterranean, to forearm her against winter, on Sept. 15, for about 3 weeks.)

Alas! in my domestic circumstances I cannot offer lodging, entertainment, or any of the normal hospitalities one would desire to offer in such a case. (I have not even a spare bedroom!). But if you were in Oxford you could have access to all the files and relevant material, and I should benefit by your opinions and assistance, especially with regard to the main problem: in what mode to present it, discussion would be (for me) a great encouragement and help.

I have, of course, made some money out of my books, though less than legend makes it, especially after the attentions of the tax-gatherers. . . .

I could not hope to remunerate you or defray your expenses in any way proper to your value! But I should wish (and insist on it) to ask you to receive some honorarium. That, however, we can go into, if I hear again that you are willing to help. I should call the Job: *editorial and critical assistance.* . . .

With my cordial wishes and very deep gratitude for your generous thought and offer,

Yours very sincerely,

J. R. R. Tolkien.

I began at once to prepare to render him the best service I could. I brushed up on mythology in general and the mythologies of northern Europe in particular. I once again, and now more carefully than ever, read *The Lord of the Rings* looking particularly for allusions to the First and Second Ages of Middle-earth. I assembled this material and gave attention to its chronology and geography.

I reached England on June 16 and called on Mr. Rayner Unwin, Tolkien's publisher, in London. I found him a cordial man with fine eyes and a great interest in Tolkien. He graciously said he hoped I might be the one to put *The Silmarillion* in shape for publication. He had recently been up to Oxford to visit Tolkien and I thought that one object of his trip might have been to persuade him to cooperate fully with me. No one knew better than he that a campaign of sorts was needed to get a manuscript out of the famous man.

But first Mr. Unwin urged me to persuade Tolkien to write a brief preface to his translations of *The Pearl* and *Sir Gawain and the Green Knight*. Tolkien wanted it to have a preface, else the translations would already have been in print, but for some years he had failed to write it. Even a very brief preface would do, Mr. Unwin assured me. Actually, in this I failed utterly. My various reminders and coaxings were accepted seriously, yet at the end of the summer Tolkien almost triumphantly said, "Well, I didn't write it!" One day, earlier in the summer, he had said, in some exasperation, (and I think mainly to himself) that he *couldn't* write it until the thing came "rightly" to him. Later I was to learn that those translations had been completed at least twenty years before and their publication continuously postponed until he could better perfect what he had undertaken.

And yet he did indeed intend to bring the task to completion. On August 10th I found him with the *Gawain* translation in hand. He assured me he expected to get it off to London "right away." Again on the 18th he was working on it with intention to complete it. On August 25th he told me that Mr. Unwin expected it by September 15th. His tone was utterly matter-of-fact and I thought he fully expected within three weeks to have the material ready. One sees a significant element of Tolkien's makeup in the fact that at his death seven years later these translations were still unpublished. Whether that preface was ever written I do not know.

I went up to Oxford and settled in at Pusey House. Then I telephoned the Tolkiens that I was at their service. I was warmly welcomed into the Professor's upstairs quarter, I found the place no less crowded than two years earlier. He was in process of revising *The Two Towers*. He began our new association by showing me boxes of manuscripts—poetic, scholarly, creative. As Time went on I discovered him a Barliman Butterbur, looking here and there for portion of *The Silmarillion*. Having had some experience in setting up filing systems, I finally offered to put his papers in order, a proposal he quickly rejected on the ground that *then* he should never find anything.

I was immediately aware that he had much unpublished writing. For instance, he was an expert on *The Ancrene Riwle*, that little book from the thirteenth century offering guidance to three women who had purposed to become nuns. He often mentioned this work and others from its time. He was also an expert in the Middle English period and once told me that he never opened a book written then without finding new things in it. He had serious thoughts of doing a translation of the Anglo-Saxon epic *Beowulf* but felt the task would be difficult because the poem was so concentrated. Coming over to me, he illustrated his concern by putting his torso almost against mine and, pulling back his fist, insisted that the reader must feel the very sword-thrust into the dragon. He said he had written parts of a bestiary, some bits of which had gone into *Tom Bombadil*. But I was aware also of numerous unmentioned manuscripts. One can imagine the perplexity of a writer with so many ideas and so many incomplete or unperfected writings on hand and with the realization of so little time left. He was then seventy-four.

Two things immediately impressed me. One was that *The Silmarillion* would never be completed. The other was the size of my own task. How could I in a few weeks read, analyze and give a critical judgment on such a mammoth literary effort? Actually I spent one entire day on a six-page section of the manuscript.

Perhaps I can best give an idea of our sessions together by a seriatim record of one of them. But first I should say that what went on was hardly a conversation. One of my friends had been told by C. S. Lewis that one might ask Tolkien questions but one would not necessarily get the answers expected. One might find him talking on an entirely different topic, to which he had seen a relationship lost to the questioner. I soon found this to be true. Discovering that efforts to discuss portions of the manuscript with him would not succeed, I began to write out my comments and simply attach them to the manuscript.

Here are the notes I made from my first day with him that summer:

1. His fan letters tend to come in waves, and he has three sorts of replies: a) a purely form letter, b) a form letter he personally signs, and infrequently c) a response dictated to his secretary.

2. He had nothing good to say about the *Saturday Evening Post* feature that had just appeared. He said that he had finally hung up on the transatlantic conversation with the author of it. But he did confess that his own mode of speaking was a factor.[1] In point of mystifying circumlocution C. S. Lewis compared Tolkien to his own father, whose conversation often contained *non sequiturs* that first bothered the hearer and then became so outrageous as to be screamingly funny. Tolkien's deviations from the expected were owing not to preoccupation but rather to his scurry after the quarry across mental fences and quagmires.

3. Looking out of his window at a birch in the front yard, he declared it to be his totem tree.

4. He and Mrs. Tolkien were angry with W. H. Auden for remarks he was reported to have made at a meeting of the Tolkien Society in Brooklyn, New York, especially his comment that the Tolkien home was "hideous...with hideous pictures on the walls."[2] Mrs. Tolkien invited me to come and sit in the same chair Auden had occupied when visiting them and see if I thought the house looked hideous. I readily confessed that it was a nicer house than I had ever lived in myself.

A little earlier Auden had agreed to write a brochure on Tolkien for a series being published in the United States. Tolkien emphatically assured me that Auden would never get his permission. He told the publisher what he had written Auden: "I regret very much to hear that you have contracted to write a book about me. It does meet with my strong disapproval. I regard such things as premature impertinences; and unless undertaken by an intimate friend, or with consultation of the subject (for which I have no time at present), I cannot believe that they have a usefulness to justify the distaste and irritation given to the victim. I wish at any rate that any book could wait until I produce *The Silmarillion.* I am constantly interrupted in this; but nothing interferes more than the present pother about 'me' and my history." It should be said, however, that Tolkien went on to express his gratitude for Auden's ardent commendation of *The Lord of the Rings.*[3] Later in the summer, Tolkien spoke to me of his hope that this disagreement with Auden might be wiped out when they got together in the autumn. Whether it was settled or not I do not know. I had the opportunity afterwards to talk with Auden and found him most friendly toward the Tolkiens.

5. He spoke of his dislike of the covers on the Ballantine paperbacks. To my surprise, he said he was glad for the Ace Books controversy because it kept Mr. Ballantine on his toes. Actually, Tolkien's general opinion of publishers was not high. He felt that even the U. S. clothback publishers did their business poorly as to distribution. As time went on he repeatedly reminded me that it was actually the Ace edition of *The Lord of the Rings* that first made him widely known, a comment curiously in opposition to the diatribes against Ace current in those days.

The whole controversy arose after Houghton Mifflin had imported unfolded press sheets from George Allen & Unwin for its U. S. Edition. The copyright laws allowed this on condition that no more than fifteen hundred copies be imported. When more than the legal number were brought in, Ace Books used this infraction as excuse to issue its paperback. This lower-priced book sold widely. Eventually the word went out that Ace had simply pirated its edition. Young admirers writing in the *Tolkien Journal* and other such periodicals were outraged. Tolkien wrote a letter to his readers in the U. S. denouncing the Ace edition and asking them not to buy it. He repeated the idea in the Foreword to the Ballantine Books paperback. But, as I have said, he told me afterwards that it was actually the Ace edition which first brought him into wide public notice. Of course there was no necessary conflict. Tolkien could appreciate the acclaim and still object to the moral angle and the loss of royalties. Ace Books had not at that time sent Tolkien any money, though they did later.

The really upsetting aspect of all this lay elsewhere. Tolkien insisted to me and to others that this controversy so occupied his time that it interfered with the completion of *The Silmarillion*. One of the deeply puzzling aspects of Tolkien comes to light in this circumstance, perhaps another a case of "contrasistency." I failed to understand why he could not see instantly that the Ace edition need not usurp even one day of his time. It was a purely legal matter and only needed to be handed over to his lawyer.

6. He was pleased with the Japanese translation of *The Hobbit* and showed me with particular satisfaction the frontispiece which portrayed Smaug falling convulsively over Dale. He had various other translations on his shelves. The Portuguese illustrations he regarded as "horrible."

7. He mentioned Mrs. Tolkien's chronic illness. He spoke proudly of his four children, one by one.

8. I asked him if people had not sought to write his biography. He said they had and went on to discuss the difference between the outward facts and the inward motives of a life, mentioning as an illustration the joys which stirred him as a child in South Africa and at his first glimpse of his "native" English soil.

9. He has the intention of completing a full account of the Second Age of Middle-earth under the title *The Akallabeth*, a word made up of *kalab* meaning "fall down," with the doubled "l" giving it intensity, i.e., the "great fall."

The Númenorean language, he informed me, is based on Hebrew.

10. He showed me many manuscripts, most of them old and obviously reworked.

I shall return later to some of these topics, but here I have simply intended to show the variety of subjects that might come up in a visit with Professor Tolkien. I might add here that Mrs. Tolkien would sometimes come in and join the conversation. She was always gracious and friendly.

I went out to their home on Sanfield Road two or three times a week and was there one to three hours, periods solidly filled with talk, nearly all his.

It was said that C. S. Lewis could make a new suit look old the second time he put it on. Not so with Tolkien. He was always neatly dressed from necktie to shoes. One of his favorite suits was a herringbone with which he wore a green corduroy vest. Always there was a vest, and nearly always a sport coat. He did not mind wearing a very broad necktie which in those days was out of style. Once he spoke admiringly of a tie I was wearing and I rewarded him with it.

The most obvious thing about him was not his clothing but his easy and stately stance and particularly his well shaped head and ever interesting face. Much of the time there was about him the atmosphere of the actor, yet without any sense of the jack-a-dandy. His conversation bore about it a steady parturiency, like the sort of grass that sends out runners to root in every direction. One often felt that his words could not pour out fast enough—there was a sense of the galloping on of all his ideas at once, along with kaleidoscopic facial changes.

In fact, I have never known anyone who so successfully meshed facial and oral expression. One noticed the built-in humor that seemed to begin around the mouth and eyes and extend back into the brain and down into the solid torso and on indefinitely. His penetrating eyes took possession of his hearer and his eyebrows lifted instantly to express a point made or the beginning of an idea to be lassoed, tied down and branded on the spot, or lowered to concentrate while conveying the assurance that behind those eyes something nimble and many-faceted was taking shape and would momentarily erupt. But it also seemed to me that at times there was a passing enjoyment over what he was keeping back in the very moment of the eruption.

Sometimes there would appear a pixy face, round and growing up toward what seemed could only end in a chuckle, yet never quite did. Or a genial face suddenly shifting into an expression of blazing criticism, soon followed by a repentant warmth. Sometimes a "What!" face and sometimes a "Yes, we can take care of that subject also" face. And always there was an expression of both pose and genuineness revealed like a double exposure. Then again (occasionally) a dead-serious face emerged like the others from deep within him along with a look through the window into nowhere, pipe held stolidly at center.

We met generally in his upstairs room but sometimes in the garage office. When the weather was warm, we might go out into the garden. On our first visit there he took me round the garden and gave me the personal history of nearly every plant, and even the grass. He said he had loved trees since childhood and pointed out the trees he had himself planted. One easily understands Michael Tolkien's remark that from his father he "inherited an almost obsessive love of trees" and considered the massing felling of trees "the wanton murder of living beings for very shoddy ends:" Tolkien wrote a letter to the editor of the London *Sunday Telegraph* taking exception to what he thought an unfair allusion to his attitude toward trees. "In all my works," he wrote, "I take the part of trees as against all their enemies" and he spoke of "the destruction, torture and murder of trees perpetrated by private individuals and minor official bodies. The savage sound of the electric saw is never silent wherever trees are still found growing."[4] He spoke of birds, saying that a certain blackbird was now tame enough to eat out of Mrs. Tolkien's hand. He recommended to me a particular book on the sparrow. Elsewhere he is reported to have said that his most treasured book was Johns' *Flowers of the Field*.[5]

It would be satisfying to record that I always found him busy at his writing, but that is not true. I did find him sometimes working at his Elvish languages, an activity which seemed endlessly interesting to him. I think he did a good deal of reading of detective stories and science-fiction. He told me more than once of his pride in being chosen a member of a science-fiction writers' association in the United States. Yet in *Tree and Leaf* he speaks of science-fiction as "that most escapist form of all literature." He said he found Dorothy Sayers a "fair" writer of detective stories but believed he found some "vulgarity" both in them and in her *Man Born to be King*. He did not care for the detective stories of G. K. Chesterton.

He was happy with what he considered his histrionic talents, saying he had done some stage work in earlier life. He had the script of a British Broadcasting Corporation dramatization of *The Lord of the Rings*, thought it badly done, that he could have acted better than some who took part, but that the BBC had refused him the chance. Those who have heard the Caedmon phonograph records in which he reads from *The Hobbit, The Lord of the Rings* and *Tom Bombadil* know the dramatic quality he sought after. One is also impressed with the melodic beauty of his reading of Elvish and also the recorded Gregorian-chant character of a longer Elvish poem sung by William Elvin to the music of Donald Swann. When I was with him he once began to read me a passage in Elvish, then stopped, came up close and placing the manuscript before me said that Elvish ought not to be read but sung and then chanted it in a slow and lovely intonation.

Tolkien's skill as an artist is now well known, particularly from the illustrations he did for *The Hobbit*. He spoke of the pleasure he had in doing the tree that appeared on the British edition of *Tree and Leaf*, also of the problem of drawing the many varieties of leaves. His readers can look forward to many other pictures done by him. He also had the mastery of various forms of handwriting. Once he sat down and wrote out my name in thirteenth-century script. His interest in medieval literature and life was more than a profession—it was a love.

He told me more than once how his grandfather, I think it was, could write the Lord's Prayer on a sixpence when he was over ninety. I got the impression that he himself expected to live to a very old age. But both he and Mrs. Tolkien were then in need of some attention from physicians. Both complained of rheumatism, which they felt was accentuated by wet weather. Sometimes he could rise from a chair only with real effort, and then would remain standing rather than sit again. One day the idea arose of our taking a walk over some path which he and Lewis had once covered, but he said it was no longer possible for him to walk far. He reminisced about earlier years when he could ride his bicycle up the long, steep Headington Hill between his home and the university.

As readers of Tolkien know, the contrast of light and darkness in *The Lord of the Rings* is always emphasized. In this connection Tolkien told me of C. S. Lewis's story about the man born with a cataract on each eye. He kept hearing people talk of light but could not understand what they meant. After an operation he had some sight but had not yet come to understand *light*. Then one day he saw the haze rising from a pond (actually, said Tolkien, the pond at the front of Lewis's home) and thought that at last he was seeing light. In his eagerness to experience real light, he rushed joyfully into it and was drowned.

I greatly hoped that Tolkien would accept an invitation to be present in Cheltenham for a dramatization under the direction of Mrs. E. M. Webster of *The Lord of the Rings*, but almost at the last minute he declined and suggested I go instead. It was one of the finest experiences of my summer, two and a half hours' presentation by ten and eleven-year-old British children who had spent part of their time for an entire year studying the story and preparing their own dialogue, scenery and costumes. The play was put on in a small gymnasium. I was given a front seat and sometimes had Gollum crawling over my feet, as the stage was small for the number of youngsters taking part—participating, I should add, with dead seriousness. I was later told that the boy who played Frodo Baggins did not emerge from his rôle for a month and then only reluctantly. It has occurred to me many times since that perhaps nothing more fitting could be done in the way of a movie version than what I saw in Cheltenham that night. More than once I was moved to tears.

One day toward the end of the summer I found Tolkien in very low spirits. He said he was too tired to think about anything. He had been up during the night with Mrs. Tolkien and said he was going tc bed for some rest. But as I rose to return to Oxford he began talking and perked up quickly. Actually gloom had little part in his make-up. Once his doctor prescribed a collar for cervical muscular spasm. When I arrived he grabbed it, put it around his neck, stuck his face into mine and asked how I would like to wear *that* in the summer heat.

One thing for which Tolkien would stop talking was to hear a good story or joke. He had a fine supply of his own. Once he spoke of getting a letter from a husband whose pregnant wife had fallen in love with Aragorn and what was he to do? Tolkien had no answer for that one. While I was there a bust of him done by his daughter-in-law was being completed. He had picked up both the plaster and bronze casts and was carrying them, one on each side, in a taxicab. It came into his scholarly head that they were like the Dioscuri twins, Castor and Pollux, but he immediately concluded that their real names should be Castor and Plaster.

Sometimes his wit was so close to both humor and reality that it was impossible to decide which he meant. He told me once that women always kill bees, moths, spiders and such creatures inside the house, but men capture the insect and carry it to a door or window and let it go free. He went on to describe how once in a dining room he had used his match box to capture a fly on a stranger's nose and how the man was surprised and a little indignant about it.

It was Mrs. Tolkien's task to stand between Ronald, as she called him, and the many visitors who sought to see him. One man showed up at their door saying, "I have traveled six thousand miles to see Professor Tolkien." She politely had told him that her husband was simply not seeing anybody. One reason might have been that he was carrying what she described as a "big covered thing" which she believed to be a tape recorder. One might as well have brought a loaded gun to the door. I felt gratified when he so willingly allowed me to take a picture of him on my earlier visit, also a couple of times on the second.

His attitude toward photographers was similar to that toward feature writers, i.e., that they were people likely to do the wrong thing. In this connection he showed me a large, elaborate book of photographs that someone had sent him. The photographer had obviously waited until his subjects could be caught in a grimace or some other un-natural appearance and had made up his book out of such distortions. Tolkien had been asked to pose but on seeing the results, congratulated himself that he had refused.

It seemed to me that, perhaps rather naturally, he had

mixed and somewhat antithetical feelings about any public image of himself. On the one hand, he was proud of seeing himself as a successful writer. I had the impression that some of his colleagues at the university (and possibly also some of his own relatives) had lifted eyebrows concerning his decades of toil over Elves and Orcs and dragons. Now all but the most cynical were put in their places and even the cynical could not fail to admit that the work, whether good or bad, had paid off financially. On the other hand, Tolkien took appreciations with a grain of salt. Like Lewis, he held a low opinion of the twentieth century, literary critics and all.[6]

Tolkien spoke of the "terrible twenties" as having laid the foundation for the collapse of later years. He felt that education at all levels was deteriorating. He believed that England's government was going from bad to worse and spoke of the leaders as "don-lets," a word which also suggested his feelings about the dons! He had little use for modern gadgets and many modern ideas. He felt nothing but antagonism for "psychological" explanations. "Nobody ever takes to psychology unless there is something wrong with his own 'psychology,' " he used to say. He was amused by Freudian interpretations of *The Hobbit* in which some of his motives were supposedly explained in terms of his being scared by spiders in his youth. On the contrary, he insisted, he and his boyhood friends scared each other with spiders because they really *liked* to be scared!

I also got the impression that many of the older writers also displeased Tolkien. He said he did not like Russian writers and could not read them. Interviewed by a London newspaper, he is reported to have said of Lewis's comparison of *The Lord of the Rings* to Ariosto, "I don't know Ariosto and I'd loathe him if I did. . . . Cervantes was a weed-killer to romance. . . . Dante doesn't attract me. He's full of spite and malice. I don't care for his petty relations with petty people in petty cities."[7] I was pleasingly surprised at the familiarity he showed with American literature, especially that of Mark Twain.

One antipathy of his struck me oddly. Though elsewhere he had spoken of George MacDonald with real appreciation, at the time I visited Tolkien he was making frequent wholesale attacks on him. He called him an "old grandmother" who preached instead of writing. He thought MacDonald would have done better to retain his native dialect in some of his writings. He did not like the way in which MacDonald wrote of trees, etc. Now there is common agreement that MacDonald's writings have serious shortcomings at their worst but equally great significance at their best. A friend of mine who is well versed in MacDonald and also fond of Tolkien suggests that the dislike of MacDonald may have arisen partly to throw people off the scent of his deep indebtedness. Whatever the real explanation, I think that the indebtedness is clear.

A similar antipathy of Tolkien's was for one of his own characters, Sam Gamgee. I have never known a reader who did not on the whole find Sam a person to be admired. Yet Tolkien spoke to me about Sam as "vulgar" and "despicable," and in a letter to Vera Chapman he described Sam as sententious and cocksure. "He was the youngest son of a stupid and conceited old peasant. Together with his loyal master-servant attitude, and his personal love for Frodo, he retains a touch of the contempt of his kind (moderated to tolerant pity) for motives above their reach."[8]

But if Tolkien was critical of others he was even more critical of his own writings. Few authors ever denigrated their own works more than he. In the Foreword to the Ballantine paperback of *The Lord of the Rings* he describes the story as containing "many defects, minor and major" and that he might well have produced an accessory volume of explanation and additions. The chief defect is actually the omission of what he obviously intended to put into the story and did not. For instance, he says there were five

Wizards but two are never again mentioned and a third is barely named. Again, Cirdan is essentially a nobody, though he held Narya the Great, one of the Three Rings of Power, and we are told "saw further and deeper than any other in Middle-earth." (III, 456) Possibly Tolkien, given more time, would have built the other three Wizards and also Cirdan into a truly noteworthy place in his story.

Something of the extent of Tolkien's perfectionism may be sensed by noting that he, like C. S. Lewis, thought a story properly composed only after the author had first done the whole thing in poetry and then turned it back into prose. Some of the manuscript of *The Silmarillion* is in verse form. It is a concept reminiscent of Horace's dictum that an author rework his writings for nine years before giving them to the public.

Yet, as I have said, Tolkien greatly disliked the image of himself as an unsubstantial dreamer. He wanted to be thought of as, in Wordsworth's phrase, "a man speaking to men." The truth is that he was sometimes impractical, not in the self-conscious manner but in the everyday one. A problem that was bothering him when I was with him involved an American manufacturer who proposed to exploit the Hobbit image by making dolls, T-shirts and the like. This manufacturer declared his intention of going ahead with or without permission but offered some remuneration for the privilege. Again I felt it to be simply a legal affair that need not at all trouble Tolkien the writer.

But another somewhat parallel problem might indeed have properly usurped his time. Young people fell in love with his Elvish languages and some of them began to discover the linguistic principles of their construction. Some in their enthusiasm proceeded to extend the Elvish to its various possible forms, and a dictionary of greater or less proportions seemed inevitable. They would have supposedly been able to copyright the very languages invented by him and thus put a check on his own use of them. I tried to reassure him that the Hobbit images and the extension of his languages were both evidences of his growing reputation and in the case of the languages could do him no real harm. As to the languages, I suggested that he might kill two birds with one stone by simply writing an entire book in Elvish. Not only would many young people love it but he could then copyright his Elvish vocabulary. He made the surprising answer that he would indeed do a story in Elvish if only he knew enough Elvish!

I became convinced that Professor Tolkien was suffering in an accentuated way, because of his genius, from some of the inner conflicts belonging to us all. I found that he had a real measure of "insecurity." As early as 1939 C. S. Lewis wrote his brother that Tolkien's "trials, besides being frequent and severe, are usually of such a complicated nature as to be impenetrable." Now internationally famous, he nevertheless needed assurance concerning himself as a writer and particularly concerning *The Silmarillion*. He had such grave and longstanding doubts about the story that I felt he had done little work on it for years, and had possibly even grown unfamiliar with it.

My own policy in the reading of other people's manuscripts, and particularly when I ask others to read my own, is to give or request negative criticism, the sort that nets the most value toward a revision. But I quickly discovered that sort of criticism was not what Tolkien wanted or needed. Convinced that he could not write a genuinely poor story, I was able conscientiously to be generous with my praise. And this I was. My negative criticism of the manuscript became more or less a footnote to the positive. Afterwards I remembered that Lewis also believed that Tolkien could be influenced only be encouragement.[9]

A similar need extended further. I was perfectly willing simply to listen to what Tolkien had to say rather than insist upon a two-way communication. In due course I discovered his need of a genuinely interested listener. Before

we had been long together he said one day that, if I
would hold it confidential, he would "put more under my
hat" than he had ever told anyone. But as time went on I
realized that any discussion of his most deeply private
world was simply impossible for him. Indeed, for a period
it seemed to me that the very idea generated its contrariety
and modified the ordinary generosity of his conversation.
As opportunity allowed I encouraged him to speak his
deepest feelings, but to no avail. Whatever he might have
revealed I have little idea, though I remain certain that he
was fundamentally "every inch a man" and a good man at
that.

His problem as a writer he stated with great charm and
meaning at the beginning of his story "Leaf by Niggle."
That story begins, "There was once a little man called
Niggle, who had a long journey to make." The journey
was into death and the hereafter. Niggle describes himself
as a painter, not a very successful one owing not only to
interruptions which usurped his time but to a tendency
toward plain laziness. Niggle's real trouble was that his
reach exceeded his grasp. He had various paintings that he
worked on and "most of them were too large and ambitious
for his skill." Actually he preferred to paint leaves more
than trees. "He used to spend a long time on a single leaf,
trying to catch its shape, and its sheen, and the glistening
of dewdrops on its edges." Yet at the same time he longed
to paint a whole tree. Indeed one painting had started
with "a single leaf caught in the wind" but it grew,
"sending out innumerable branches, and thrusting out the
most fantastic roots. Strange birds came and settled on
the twigs and had to be attended to." For me it represents
both a splendid picture of his perfectionism and the
increasing vision of the mythology he was creatively to
inhabit.

But then came a larger idea still. Not just a single leaf, nor
only a tree, but an entire country began to show up, in-

cluding high mountains in the far distance. Niggle now turned away from his other paintings "or else he took them and tacked them on to the edges of his great picture." Might this not explain the Tom Bombadil episode and the Bombadil poems that did not quite manage to get into the main story? In due course Niggle's painting got so large he needed a ladder to reach its top. What a perfect insight into the whole creative process, whether Tolkien's or that of a Thomas Wolfe, a Stephen Spender, or any creative mind overwhelmed by the magnitude of its subject.

The time eventually came when Niggle began to take a hard look at what was turning out to be the main activity of his life. He looked and looked and wished for someone who "would tell him what to think." He wondered if he were simply wasting time. He wondered if he should have dropped all other paintings for this single one. Was it really a painting, or was it just a chimera? Niggle concluded contradictory things about it. "Actually it seemed to him wholly unsatisfactory, and yet very lovely, the only really beautiful picture in the world." Not only do we have here the experience of many a writer or artist, but we have what seems a most faithful description of Tolkien's own creativity.

In the Foreword to the Ballantine edition, Tolkien begins by saying, "This tale grew in the telling, until it became a history of the Great War of the Ring and included many glimpses of the yet more ancient history that preceded it." And what a landscape is seen! Yet the greatest defect of *The Lord of the Rings*, said he, is that it is too short. I can easily believe that Tolkien, had he had enough lives, would have written thirty or forty thousand pages, and who knows whether it would not still have been too short for his teeming genius?

I might remark on one apparent difference between Niggle and his counterpart. Niggle was up on his ladder at work when the Inspector in black came to take him away.

My own impression was that Tolkien, despite protestations to the contrary, had greatly slowed down at the time of my visit and perhaps seldom climbed the ladder clear to the top at all. I hope I am wrong. And even if I am right, might not a Niggle at seventy-four richly deserve a recess from the heights?

Some Notes on "Smith of Wootton Major"

Though the reading of *The Silmarillion* was proving about as much as I could handle during that summer of 1966, Tolkien from time to time handed me other shorter pieces and asked me about their publishability. One was called "The Bovadium Fragments," a satire written long before and having as its main point the worship of the *Motores*, i.e., automobiles, and the traffic jams blocking the roads in and around Oxford. It was full of the inventiveness to be expected of Tolkien. Some of the characters are Rotzopny, Dr. Gums, and Sarevelk. I judged that it had two elements that would make it unpublishable. One was the more than liberal use of Latin, and the other the probability that a reader's eye would focus on its playfulness rather than its serious implications. Actually it was an early comment on the commercialization of our world.

The other and far more interesting manuscript was *Smith of Wootton Major*. I assured him it was my notion that it should be published as soon as possible. It actually was published in 1967, but whether my recommendation had anything to do with it I am doubtful.

In order to comment on this story, it is necessary for me to remark once again that while I was with him Tolkien frequently fired verbal cannonades at George MacDonald. Someone had asked Tolkien to consider writing an introduction to a book on MacDonald and he had for that reason gone back to read again some of his works. He said he had found MacDonald terrible and his broadside criticism of him implied that nothing he had written was worthwhile. I asked Tolkien if *Smith of Wootton Major* referred to MacDonald. No, he said, his aversion had only been the "explosion" that started him off on the story, no more.

I read the story and interpreted it as primarily about the creative process and the special problems of a fantasy writer like Tolkien. He staunchly denied it had any autobiographical meaning. It was, he said, originally intended as "just a story about cake." But it still occurred to me that at the beginning Old Nokes may represent MacDonald. "Fairies and sweets were two of the very few notions he had about the tastes of children." Nokes knew the sort of things that should be outside a cake but had dim notions as to "the inside of a Great Cake" and so went to some old recipe books of former cooks and also hunted up some spices. In this search he found a much tarnished star.

Nokes thought the star "funny" and therefore amusing to children, but his young apprentice, who was actually a far better cook, insisted it was *faërie* and a serious business. Here we seem to have a fundamental idea from Tolkien's essay "On Fairy-stories," and if Nokes is meant to be MacDonald we must assume that Tolkien thought his "faërie" simply something pretty and sweet with little notion of eucatastrophe and evangelium. (I can imagine lovers of MacDonald rising up wrathfully to dispute this conception. I myself would dispute it.)

The star, along with other trinkets, was baked into the cake, and at the winter festival the ten-year-old son of the smith swallowed it unknowingly. But the star possessed faërie and so the child sang "high and clear, in strange words that he seemed to know by heart." The child began to be almost the opposite of the stodgy Nokes and even of his community. He became a good workman, making useful things but also at times beautiful and substantial ones as well. But because too many people were like Old Nokes, he could speak of faërie to few.

Some few at least could understand what was taking place in young Smith, yet no one understood the beauty and terror he experienced on some of his longer journeys. Eventually "possessed," Smith saw "elven mariners tall and terrible." Smith also strayed in grey mists and over wide plains. Finally he found the "King's tree ... tower upon tower ... and it bore at once leaves and flowers and fruits uncounted, and not one was the same as any other that grew on the Tree." Though Smith never saw that tree again, he could never forsake the search, and the search led him through "the Vale of Evermorn" and glory where he heard elven voices and found maidens dancing.

It seems to me that the autobiography is unmistakable. The star unconsciously swallowed suggests the manner in which creativity rises in seemingly accidental fashion and without precedent. The useful things he at first made could represent Tolkien's scholarship. Later came his vision of Middle-earth. I suspect that such a vision almost inevitably meets with skepticism, if not outright derision, among the other makers of "useful" things, not to mention the vast multitude who are non-makers. The beauty and terror seen by Smith on his longer journeys clearly represent, I believe, Tolkien's particular birth into the world of myth and his own "calling" to the myth of Middle-earth, a calling which is intensified by the visits to elvish country and the tree bearing "leaves and flowers and fruits uncounted." (How close this is to *Tree and Leaf*!) This created world is to be as large as the world itself.

In the story Smith, when he returned home, seemed more of an oddity than ever to his neighbors. But he bore a light that had been given him by a fairy Queen. She told him not to be too much ashamed of his own folk. And here the story may return to MacDonald. Old Nokes had wanted to stick "a little doll on a pinnacle in the middle of the Cake, dressed all in white, with a little wand in her hand ending in a tinsel star, and Fairy Queen written in pink icing round her feet." Does Tolkien mean that though MacDonald knows nothing about the real inside of a cake, nevertheless he may accomplish something by the saccharine figures he presents? Nokes grew old and skinny and "just made his century: the only memorable thing he ever achieved." MacDonald died in 1905.

But Tolkien may also mean that the little imitation fairy had somehow incited Smith on his perilous way to find the true Queen. There is no doubt in my mind that, whatever this story may satirically say of MacDonald, and in spite of Tolkien's several severe attacks on him in my presence, Tolkien was as I have already said, clearly indebted to MacDonald. For instance, there are at least a dozen places in *The Hobbit* or *The Lord of the Rings* that are reminiscent of *The Princess and Curdie*. The most striking of them is the parallel rehabilitation of the king of Gwyntystorm and King Théoden in *The Two Towers* after a close "friend" in the palace had almost destroyed him.

I shall conclude this chapter with a note on the correspondence between us after I returned home. In October, 1966, he wrote me of "nearly seventeen days of unbroken sunshine" on a cruise he and Mrs. Tolkien had completed in the Mediterranean. It was marred, however, by the fact that Mrs. Tolkien had slipped and fallen on the first day and thereafter had been in the hands of the ship's surgeon much of the time, preventing some of the sightseeing they had anticipated. He had returned to England to a large "mound" of correspondence. In December, 1967, he wrote me that his work had proceeded "hardly at all" for a year. "I have been so distracted by business and family affairs (interlocked), and my dear wife's health, which doesn't improve, that there seems little time for concentration except at night, and I can no longer burn so much of the wrong end of the candle as I used to." In the same envelope was another letter which, said he, "I began at some date I cannot remember." He told of an illness he had experienced which was serious enough "to require the daily visits of an anxious doctor for a month, and left me an emaciated wreck. It was eight weeks before I could walk about."

Other letters passed between us in 1968 but I shall mention only one in June of that year. "I am now leaving Oxford," he wrote, "and going to live on the south coast. . . . For my own protection I shall remove my address from all books of reference or other lists." He reported that thereafter his correspondence would come through his publisher in London. "I have made up my mind not to see anybody from your country whom I do not already know, nor anybody from any Press in any country." In this letter he made a scathing reference to William Ready, the author of a book about him and reported that Ready had "the impertinence to send me a personally inscribed copy."

After Mrs. Tolkien's death late in November, 1971, he returned to his old haunts in Oxford. The pressure from visitors began to mount again. In February, 1973, I wrote him concerning the possibility of his coming to the United States to receive the honorary degree he had been offered. I suggested that if he felt able I would arrange a few speaking engagements for him and meantime do my best to guarantee such privacy as he might wish. He answered that he was unable to accept. "My age alone is I think sufficient reason but I have been in medical hands recently and have had some severe advice with regard to my future conduct." Of his life between that time and September 2, when the Inspector in black came for him, I know little.

POSTSCRIPT. Looking back at my summer with Professor Tolkien, I remember more vividly than anything else his invariable practice of coming downstairs and out to the front gate with me and always with expressions of warmest appreciation. He said that he had wanted an "outsider" to examine *The Silmarillion*, and though he had confessed his own lack of confidence in it, he showed great gratitude for what he described as a renewed interest in completing the story. The correspondence I have just mentioned unhappily suggests that apparently he did little or nothing about it. Let us all hope I am mightily wrong.

Chronology of Composition

At Tolkien's death his story of the First Age of Middle-earth was incomplete—how incomplete nobody will ever know. For him *The Lord of the Rings* was likewise unfinished. We must never fail to recognize that he was not simply "writing a story" but wrestling with a world. There is some parallel between what Tolkien was attempting and the production of Dr. Samuel Johnson's dictionary in the eighteenth century. Imagine the task of sitting down to bring together all the words of the English people and showing their pronunciation, their origin, history, usage, and varied meanings. Both Tolkien and Dr. Johnson had some precedents. There were dictionaries before Johnson and there were mythologies before Tolkien. Johnson had in view the pulling together of the world of words to provide a broad and consistent framework for the English language. Tolkien, having tried to pull together strands from the world of mythology and finding the result uneven, even weak, was endeavoring to construct a more complete pattern. He told me that he had contemplated dedicating *The Silmarillion* to Queen Elizabeth and saying, "The only thing in which your country is not rich is mythology." But perhaps no mythology whatever was as rich as Tolkien wanted it to be.

It was my task to read the typescripts which he handed me and give him my judgment of them. But I soon realized that I was doing more. Tolkien needed someone not so much to give him literary criticism as to press him, one way or another, into renewed attention to it. I have mentioned my feeling that he had done relatively little work on this story for a long time. On more than one occasion I found him unable to answer specific questions about the contents of *The Silmarillion*. He seemed happy that I was making records of what the story contained and was comparing its narrative with people and events in *The Lord of the Rings*, feeling that such a record would be valuable in the process which he described as "writing backwards." For a man of his age it was a superlunary task to set about integrating the three ages of Middle Earth into one whole.

Something of the enormity of his intention is apparent in his plan for a whole series of languages, any one of which might require decades to work out. He planned a Dwarf language. Compared with Elvish it was to sound "cumbrous and unlovely." We know of Tolkien's relish for genealogies, chronologies and maps, and of course all these were to accompany all three ages. He had drawn a splendid map of Beleriand (though in some minor ways it was incomplete) but whether there were also maps of the region of Valinor and Eressëa I do not know. I pointed out to him the good effect of poetry in *The Lord of the Rings* and the desirability of poetry in his accounts of the other ages.

What I actually did was carry to my room the portions of the story handed me and endeavor to judge them individually and in relation to each other. All together this amounted to twenty-eight portions from a couple of pages in length up to 132 pages. Sometimes there were overlapping portions. For the most part they were concerned less with the Valar and early history of Middle-earth than with Elves, Dwarves and Men, particularly Elves and more particularly the curse upon the Noldor.

In my hopes of encouraging him to go on with the composition, I pointed out with serious concern that I had found nothing about Tom Bombadil, the Ents and Entwives, the making of the Palantíri, etc. We recall, for instance, that Treebeard's eyes were "filled up with ages of memory and long, slow, steady thinking" (II, 83), and that Tom Bombadil remembered the first raindrop and the first acorn (I, 182). We are told exactly that the Ents were known to the Eldar "in ancient days" (III, 510). In my working out of a chronology for the First Age I tried to encourage him by inserting such corollaries at points which seemed to me appropriate.

The most persistent hope among readers of Tolkien is for the publication of *The Silmarillion*. What many of them do not recognize is that much of that story is already scattered through *The Lord of the Rings*. There are over six hundred allusions to the First and Second Ages of Middle-earth in *The Hobbit* and *The Lord of the Rings*, all the way from the times before time when Eru, the One, creator of all things and self-existent, gave a vision of all Arda to the heavenly beings about him, to Eärendil's desperate voyage centuries later to the Blessed Realm to request help from the Valar lest Middle-earth be entirely overcome by Morgoth (I, 308-311). The appendices to Vol. III are, in places, rich with significant information. In the story proper we may expect to find allusions particularly germane to the Elves in the songs and tales of such places as Rivendell, Lothlórien and Fangorn. A Dwarf such as Gimli may be expected to allude warmly to the past in locations like Moria and Helm's Deep. Mysterious intuitions of the ancient past may also come from a Hobbit such as Sam Gamgee. Allusions to the Second Age are more likely in such places as Rohan and Gondor. In truth, past history pervades the stories of Tolkien that are already in print, and careful reading of those accounts often reveals not simply the facts but often the poignant joys, sorrows and significance of those ages.

I must leave my reader the choice either of making his own reconstruction of *The Silmarillion* out of *The Lord of the Rings* and other books by Tolkien or else the easier way of simply awaiting the publication of that story. What I wish to do now is discuss briefly the chronology of the composition of Tolkien's fiction.

Unless one reads with care it is possible to assume that most of Tolkien's creative writing was done in the 1930s and later. In the Foreword to the Ballantine paperback of *The Lord of the Rings* Tolkien says that this story was "begun soon after *The Hobbit* was written and before its publication in 1937." He adds that the content of *The Lord of the Rings* was derived in some of its elements from what had been said in *The Hobbit*. Indeed, its main theme, the Ring, was settled with the finding of the ring by Bilbo at the time of his underground riddle-making contest with Gollum and his knowledge of the fact that it made the wearer invisible.

Tolkien goes on to say that after the publication of *The Hobbit* in 1937 he was "encouraged by requests by readers for more information concerning hobbits and their adventures" and this caused him to go back to "the older world," i.e., to such characters and places as Gandalf, the High-elves, Durin, Moria, Elrond and Gondolin. It was the "discovery of the significance of these glimpses and of their relation to the ancient histories [which] revealed the Third Age and its culmination in the War of the Ring."

He continues in this Foreword to say that "the composition of *The Lord of the Rings* went on at intervals during the years 1936 to 1949," and he identifies particular portions and the year of their composition. In a letter he reports, "The general idea of *The Lord of the Rings* was certainly in my mind from an early stage; that is from the first draft of Book I, Chapter 2, written in the 1930's. From time to time

I made rough sketches or synopses of what was to follow, immediately or far ahead; but these were seldom of much use: the story unfolded itself as it were. The tying-up was achieved, so far as it is achieved, by constant re-writing backwards."[10] Book I, Chapter 2 recounts Gandalf's long talk with Frodo about his search for Gollum and the meaning of the Ring, now vastly larger than in *The Hobbit*, so one can see how very naturally the writing of that portion came first.

But in his article in *Diplomat* Tolkien proposes an entirely different version of the origin and composition of his main creative works. "This business," he said, "began so far back that it might be said to have begun at birth." The mythology "first began to take shape during the 1914-18 war. *The Fall of Gondolin* (and the birth of Eärendil) was written in Hospital and on leave after surviving the Battle of the Somme in 1916." Very significantly, he speaks of the account of Lúthien Tinúviel and Beren as the "kernel" of the mythology, and says that it arose from a "small woodland glade filled with 'hemocks' (or other white unbellifers) near Roos in the Holderness peninsula—to which I occasionally went when free from regimental duties while in the Humber Garrison in 1913."[11] Actually he told one of his closest friends that he had the whole of his mythic world in his mind as early as 1906. He told me that he was writing some of *The Silmarillion* (doubtless yet untitled) about 1910, and he wrote me that the story, meaning possibly the account as a whole, began in 1916-1917 "and has been with me ever since."[12]

I think it unwise to understand anything other than that all three ages of Middle-earth, and indeed *The Hobbit*, have, in some respects at least, a cognate fountainhead in Tolkien's imagination.

As early as January, 1930, Lewis identified Tolkien to Arthur Greeves in Ireland as "the writer of the voluminous unpublished metrical romances and of the maps, companions to them, showing the mountains of Dread and Nargothrond the city of the Orcs." If by 1930 it was "voluminous," and if we recall that Tolkien was a busy don, and also that Niggle was a deliberate and painstaking artist, it is easily possible to assume an accumulaion reaching back into the 1920s or even earlier.

From a letter by Lewis to Greeves we also know the date at which *The Hobbit* was completed, for he wrote on January 30, 1930, "I have had a delightful time reading a childhood story which Tolkien has just written."[13] By 1939 Lewis reported his and Tolkien's reading together, chapter by chapter, of the "new *Hobbit*," and again in 1946 he reported that the longer story was being read a chapter at a time in the Inklings. Lewis repeatedly pointed out to people that *The Lord of the Rings* was written before the events of World War II and the use of the atomic bomb.[14] Likewise, said Lewis, it is wrong to assume that Tolkien's "methodology" grew out of the writing of *The Hobbit*. At some date after 1944, Lewis wrote Charles A. Brady that *The Hobbit* was "merely the adaptation to children of part of a huge private mythology of a most serious kind." Later Lewis called *The Hobbit* a "fragment" of *The Lord of the Rings*.[15]

This second explanation of the period of commencement of Tolkien's myth coincides with the impression I received from him. It appeared to me as we talked together that the whole thing had begun, as he says, at birth. I sometimes felt it was almost *prenatal*. The distinguishing word in a comparison of the Foreword of the Ballantine paperback and his article in *Diplomat* is "composition," i.e., the time of the pulling together of the parts into a publishable whole.

Tolkien told me that some of the poems in *Tom Bombadil* had been written by him "as a boy." He said also that his love of languages began when he was five or six, and we are told that it was his linguistic concern that generated his myth. At the beginning of his essay "On Fairy-stories" he says that he has been a lover of this sort of writing "since I learned to read." At King Edward's School in Birmingham, which he entered in 1903 at the age of eleven, he was introduced to Chaucer and Anglo-Saxon. One reason he was not a top scholar there was because much of his time was spent in private investigations of Gothic, Anglo-Saxon and Welsh as well as early attempts to invent a language of his own.

In the *Diplomat* article he makes the significant remark that ". . . the mythology (and associated languages) first began to take shape during the 1914-18 war." He told me that he had read "The Fall of Gondolin" to a college group in 1918. When I inquired about "The Lay of Eärendil," he said that there was none; that as an undergraduate he had written a few lines, but that was all.

From these statements we are able to work out a sequence of genesis and composition something like the following:

1. He acknowledged a very early love of Faërie.

2. At five or six he began to appreciate words as words, and before he entered college he was vitally involved with languages and had started to create one of his own.

3. He had written boyhood verse, some of it possibly about Tom Bombadil.

4. By 1906 he had in his mind the outline of his myth as a whole.

5. Some of the adventures of Lúthien Tinúviel were conceived by 1913.

6. By 1930 the story is "voluminous," suggesting perhaps a decade or more of sporadic composition.

7. When the story of the Valar, the earliest part of *The Silmarillion*, was composed we do not know. Yet we have Tolkien's word that as early as 1913 the long episode of Lúthien and Beren was shaping up. If that episode included the wresting of the Silmaril from Morgoth, then the Silmaril suggests the Two Trees and they in turn suggest

the Valar and the early history of Middle-earth.

8. Tolkien gave me the impression of having conceived of Hobbits not long before *The Hobbit* was written, about 1929.

9. He identified 1936 to 1945 as the period of the composition of *The Lord of the Rings*. But Lewis's assertion that that story had no connection with Hitler and the atomic bomb suggests that the essential story was in existence before the beginning of World War II in 1939.

10. In 1939 Tolkien and Lewis were reading the chapters of *The Lord of the Rings* together, perhaps each chapter as it was completed. This writing and revision were going on also in 1945 or 1946 when chapters were read to the Inklings.

11. The three volumes of *The Lord of the Rings* were published in 1954, 1955, and 1956.

12. Tolkien told me that he had "recently" written "The Wanderings of Húrin," a long account of a man captured and held by Morgoth for twenty-eight years, and of his later wanderings, a portion of *The Silmarillion*.

In the future we shall no doubt have a much better record of the chronology of the conception and composition of Tolkien's mythology, but for the present this would appear to be roughly correct.

The Geography of Middle-earth

There is no doubt at all that by interpretation, i.e., figuratively, Middle-earth represents our own world. We are at home in its struggles and its joys. The size or oddity of its inhabitants, even in the case of the Ents, does not prevent our full, and often intense, understanding of their mortal meaning. But the question is often asked whether Middle-earth is strictly related in a geographical way to our own world. This is something more than a theoretical question, for if it becomes clear that given locations are identifiable as our own then the allegorical flag may promptly begin to wave.

A good many readers believe that the Shire is England or a portion of England, and this Tolkien confirmed when I once asked him if there were Hobbits in the earlier ages. He plainly answered that there were none because Hobbits were English, a remark which both confirms geographical delineations and has wide temporal implications. As to the geography, we were once driving a few miles east of Oxford on the London Road and Tolkien pointed out little hills to the north of us that, he said, were just right for Hobbit territory. He spoke also about the old mill at Birmingham, where he lived as a boy, as being the Shire mill, and was pleased with the notion that it might for that reason be preserved.

Of course the rural charm of the Shire fits well with Tolkien's love of the English countryside. He says that the dry and barren places he had known in South Africa gave him a special power "to savour the delicate English flowers and grass."[16] The great number of Anglo-Saxon person and place names also fits both Tolkien's scholarship and his loves. Tolkien points out that though the shape of lands was much changed, Hobbits still linger in "the North-West of the Old World, east of the sea" (I, 21).

But if England is indeed Shire country, then what of the rest of Middle-earth? In a telephone conversation with Tolkien, Mr. Henry Resnick asked what was east of Rhûn and south of Harad, to which Tolkien replied, "Rhûn is the Elvish word for east. Asia, China, Japan, and all the things which people in the West regard as far away. And south of Harad is Africa, the hot countries." Then Mr. Resnick asked, "That makes Middle-earth Europe, doesn't it?" To which Tolkien replied, "Yes, of course—Northwestern Europe... where my imagination comes from."[17] Not long afterwards, when I mentioned this interview to Tolkien, he denied having ever said these things. Yet later, when in my own efforts to get the geography of *The Silmarillion* straight

I asked Tolkien where Numenor was, he promptly responded, "In the middle of the Atlantic." Is this another instance of the Professor's "contrasistency," or is there a logical explanation? He is reported to have said specifically that Mordor "would be roughly in the Balkans."[18]

All this thrusts upon us not simply geography but European history, and the allegorical framework which Tolkien so vociferously denied. For instance, shall we not under these circumstances take a new look at the degradation of the Shire during the absence of the four Hobbits and the cleansing and rehabilitation that became necessary? To localize a story geographically or temporally is always at least a threat which undercuts any larger meaning, certainly a mythic one.

IV

Tolkien as Christian Writer

A publisher's list speaks of Tolkien as "a retired Oxford Theologist." The error suggests a truth. I do not recall a single visit I made to Tolkien's home in which the conversation did not at some point fall easily into a discussion of religion, or rather Christianity. He told me that he had many times been given a story as an answer to prayer. Mrs. Tolkien joined him in remarking that one of their children had been cured, as they firmly believed, of a heart ailment, through prayer. He commonly referred to Christ as "our Lord" and was much upset when he heard others address God as though He were the Lord Mayor. C. S. Lewis says that his talks with Tolkien were a large factor in his conversion to Christianity.[19] Tolkien was a staunchly conservative Tridentine Roman Catholic.

Tolkien did indeed have a special reverence for the Virgin Mary. One of his observations was that she must have jealously guarded her pregnancy since had it been discovered Mary would either have been stoned as an adulteress or, if she had tried to explain, stoned for blasphemy.

He thought Mary must have been eager to leave Nazareth for Bethlehem and would have urged Joseph on as fast as possible. He was moved by the degradation of the birth of Christ in a stable with its filth and manure and saw it as a symbol of the real nature of holy things in a fallen world. He spoke of his special regard for the book of Luke because that writer included so much about women.

It is known that Tolkien collaborated in the preparation of the Jerusalem Bible by translating the book of Job into English from what he called a bad literal French version. His keen sense of rightness led him to learn a considerable amount of Hebrew preparatory to his task. Mrs. Mary Cawte reports attending a seminar of four pupils taught by Tolkien on the Anglo-Saxon text of the book of Exodus on which he was working in the early 1940s.

When I spoke of his success as teacher, scholar and creative writer, he responded that he had been blessed with a sense of the human, i.e., a "blessing" had preceded and entered into any real value in his life. Like Lewis, he held that theories of man's origin, physiology and mentality did not go back far enough. Psychologists, he said, sometimes explain spiritual things simply as a result of the function of the glands, failing to realize that God also made the glands.

He believed that creativity itself is a gift of God. After years of teaching aesthetics, I cannot but conclude that the whole of that difficult subject is comprehended in a single line from Tolkien's "On Fairystories": *we make still by the law in which we're made.* That he was thinking not of a merely natural origin is evidenced by the same essay where he says that "God redeemed the corrupt making-creatures" and that the Gospels resemble fairy-stories in their far-flung intimations of an unearthly Joy. "The Birth of Christ is the eucatastrophe of Man's history. The Resurrection is the eucatastrophe of the story of the Incarnation. This story begins and ends in joy." The successful fairy-story has "the very taste of primary truth" and symbolizes God's gift to man of creativity. The "Great Eucatastrophe" is the final redemption of man as declared in the Scriptures. Man is called to Joy and his ability to create "Faërie" confirms that calling. "God is the Lord, of angels, and of man—and of Elves. Legend and History have met and fused."[20] If we recall that by Tolkien's definition his own major creative writings fall within his category of fairy-stories, then it is wrong to describe them, as some have done, as pagan, pre-Christian, or anything else than what he himself held them to be.

It is true that the word "God" never appears in any of Tolkien's stories, not even in *Leaf by Niggle* where some Christian implications are overwhelming, including a conversation between God and Christ. We recall Tolkien's insistence that his story had no allegorical meaning, religious or otherwise, but contrariwise, at a later time, he spoke of invocations to Elbereth Gilthoniel and added, "These and other references to religion in *The Lord of the Rings* are frequently overlooked."[21] It seems to be another case of Tolkien's "contrasistency." Of course it is equally true that Lewis omits the use of the name of God in books which nobody can doubt as being straightforwardly Christian. I think we shall be near the truth if we conclude that the fiction of both Tolkien and Lewis is Christian, even though we recall a clear difference of opinion between them as to how explicit that meaning should be.

Not long after I began my work with Professor Tolkien, he and Mrs. Tolkien went away for a short vacation, during which he sent me a paper called "Kingship, Priesthood and Prophecy in *The Lord of the Rings*," written by a professor in New South Wales. This paper proposed that Tolkien's story was one of the most misunderstood works of modern fiction because its critics were so often unacquainted with the Bible. The writer insisted that the story is based on the manner of Christ's redemption of the world. Middle-earth is saved, he argued, through the priestly self-sacrifice of the hobbit Frodo, "the Lamb whose only real strength is his capacity to make an offering of himself." It is saved also by the wisdom of Gandalf, "the major prophet figure," as well as by the mastery of Aragorn, who begins despised and ends as King. As each agent responds to his "calling," he grows in power and grace. This essay concluded: "At every point, the human dynamics of *The Lord of the Rings* are drawn from the tradition ascribed to Christ's redemptive activity, and once this is perceived, the way is opened to an informed critical approach to the work in question." I suspect this is the sort of interpretation upon which some readers of Tolkien might look with horror.

Tolkien wrote me his own opinion: "Much of this is true enough—except, of course, the general impression given (almost irresistibly in articles having this analytical approach, whether by Christians or not) that I had any such 'schema' in my conscious mind before or during the writing." No doubt Tolkien would have agreed with C. S. Lewis's conclusion that the deeper meaning of a story must rise from the writer's lifetime spiritual roots rather than be consciously inserted.[22]

Responding to a letter from Father Robert Murray suggesting Tolkien's story impressed him as entirely about grace, Tolkien wrote: "I know exactly what you mean by the order of grace; and of course by your references to Our Lady, upon which all my own small perception of beauty both in majesty and simplicity is founded. *The Lord of the Rings* is of course a fundamentally religious and Catholic work; unconsciously so at first but consciously in the revision. I . . . have cut out practically all references to anything like "religion," to cults and practices in the imaginary world. For the religious element is absorbed into the story and the symbolism. However that is very clumsily put, and sounds more self-important than I feel. I should chiefly be grateful for having been brought up since I was eight in a faith that has nourished me and taught me all the little that I know; and that I owe my mother, who clung to her conversion and died young, largely through the hardships of poverty resulting from it."[23]

In *The Pilgrim's Regress*, Lewis depicts the universality of sin through the fiction of a farmer and his wife who come to enjoy the taste of wild apples so much that they graft branches from the original tree onto all other trees and finally all edibles whatever. Tolkien's imagery of fallen man is much the same, i.e., that the devil is in the very earth under our feet and some of him gets into the cauliflower and everything else that grows. Tolkien also believed in the *anima naturaliter christiana*, the sense of God and responsibility to Him inborn in mankind. He was greatly disturbed by the decline of Christian belief in England and elsewhere. While I was with him the news came of the murder of fourteen people by a demented student shooting from the top of a building in Texas. He said he heard this news while at breakfast and that it upset his stomach.

In the early part of this book I quoted a letter from Professor Tolkien which happened to reach me on Christmas Eve. But I did not there include a footnote to that letter which reads as follows: "I hope that perhaps this may reach you at or about Christmas. 'Lux fulgebat super nos. *Ēalā Eärendel engla beorhtast ofer middengeard monnum sended.*' Cynewulf's words from which ultimately sprang the whole of my mythology." Professor Colin Hardie tells me that the Latin phrase may have come from a medieval hymn or the like or else may simply be Tolkien's own. The meaning of it is similar to the meaning of the Anglo-Saxon from Cynewulf's *Christ*, a poem about the Advent, the Ascension and the Last Judgment, and a work with which Tolkien would have been intimately familiar. Later, at my request, Tolkien gave me his own literal translation as "Here Eärendel, brightest of angels, sent from God to men." That the full meaning of the passage may be clear, I cite the following translated passage from Cynewulf's poem, beginning with Tolkien's quotation:

> Lo! Thou Splendor of the dayspring, fairest of angels sent to men upon earth, Thou Radiance of the Sun of Righteousness, bright beyond the stars, Thou of Thy very self dost illumine all the tides of time! Even as Thou, God begotten of God, Son of the true Father, didst ever dwell without beginning in the glory of heaven, so Thine own handiwork in its present need imploreth Thee with confidence that Thou send us the bright sun, and come in Thy very person to enlighten those who have long been covered with murky cloud, and sitting here in darkness and eternal night, shrouded in sins, have been forced to endure the shadow of death.... God appeared among us without sin; the mighty Son of God and the Son of Man dwelt together in harmony among mankind.[24]

The word "Eärendel" (now spelled *Eärendil*) is well known to Tolkien readers as the brightest star in the heavens of Middle-earth. Its counterpart in our world is Venus, the Morning Star. Cynewulf's "dayspring" comes from a Biblical allusion to the birth of Christ (Luke 1:78). Knowing that it was from such a context that "the whole" of Tolkien's mythology rose, can we any longer doubt its profound Christian associations?

I have elsewhere discussed some of the Christian implications of *The Lord of the Rings*—such as descriptions of paradisal peace and splendor, the contrast between darkness and light, the sense of the ongoing of evil, Frodo's calling and dedication, the place of the human will in goodness, Christ images, the apocalyptic ending and what Tolkien calls the Eucatastrophe and Evangelium—and shall not repeat them here.[25] But there does seem abundant evidence for W. H. Auden's statement that the "unstated presuppositions" of *The Lord of the Rings* are Christian, also Edmund Fuller's conviction that, "A theology contains the narrative rather than being contained by it. Grace is at work abundantly in the story" and all the way "a thread of prophecy is being fulfilled;" also W. D. Norwood's remark in his interpretation of Tolkien's aesthetic theory that this writer "sees in the story of Christ a record of absolute reality incarnate in history."[26] Various other interpreters, though by no means all, express similar opinions.

Professor Tolkien talked to me at some length about the use of the word "holy" in *The Silmarillion*. Very specifically he told me that the "Secret Fire sent to burn at the heart of the World" in the beginning was the Holy Spirit.[27] He described his problem in depicting the fall of mankind near the beginning of the story. "How far we have fallen!" he exclaimed—so far, he felt, that it would seem impossible even to find an adequate prototype or to imagine the contrast between Eden and the disaster which followed.

I only wish that at this point I felt able to discuss the pattern of Tolkien's myth in relation to the whole of mythology. There is no doubt of its general similarity in such archetypes as a creator, a creation, a "high" race and a hierarchy, protagonists and antagonists, a sense of doom, heroic undertakings, conduct measured in terms of moral law, and an ending with a new earth and heaven. There are many discussions which endeavor to decide whether myth originates in history, religion, nature, the imaginations of men or all of these.

My impression is that *The Silmarillion* is oriented as much on a Biblical pattern as it is on that of Norse and other mythologies. One interesting instance of this is the depiction of light in Middle-earth before the creation of sun and moon, following the model of the early verses of Genesis. Many believe there was, as in *The Silmarillion*, a long period of time between the two kinds of light. Milton's explanation in *Paradise Lost* is an example:

> *"Let there be Light!" said God; and forthwith Light*
> *Ethereal, first of things, quintessence pure,*
> *Sprung from the Deep, and from her native East*
> *To journey through the aery gloom began,*
> *Sphered in a radiant cloud—for yet the Sun*
> *Was not; she in a cloudy tabernacle*
> *Sojourned the while. (VII, 243249)*

The Two Trees in *The Silmarillion* are at first the source of light. After the destruction of the Two Trees there is a long period of twilight in Middle-earth and it is during this time that first Elves and then Dwarves awaken. It is only long afterwords, with the rising of sun and moon, that Men awaken.

We are told that God saw His labors of creation to be "very good" and that on the seventh day He rested (Genesis 2:2). In a quite similar fashion the Valar enjoyed the splendor of their work and when it was completed they also rested and celebrated with a great feast.

In the beginning Eru gave the Valar a vision in heaven of Arda and required them to make it according to that vision. A parallel may be seen in God's command to Moses concerning the Jewish Tabernacle: "See that you make everything according to the pattern which was shown you on the mountain (Hebrews, 5:5).

Again, the marriage of three High Elves with Men is in some ways like the Biblical account of how "the sons of God saw the daughters of men that they were fair; and they took them wives" (Genesis 6:2). Except for a reversal in sex, this is very similar to the marriage of King Thingol the Elf to Melian the Vala (III, 388).

A major parallel between the Bible and *The Silmarillion* is a great Fall, in both cases premeditated if not actually begun in heaven and descending finally to a vast and devilish opposition against everything heavenly. The curse and its aftermath upon the Noldor suggests the Old Testament motif of disobedience and its dire results. Likewise, I think, there may be something of a parallel between Eärendil's desperate voyage to Valinor for aid from the destruction of Beleriand (and the consequent succor and warm invitation to return to that protected and lovely land) and the record of the Hebrews returning to their own land after long exile in Persia, rebuilding the temple and, after years of neglect, re-affirming the laws of Moses and sobbing out their repentance (Nehemiah 8). There are those, indeed, who believe the Jews are still fighting "the long defeat" and have yet to face their eucatastrophe.

If one presses the matter, he may find other significant parallels. The life-span of some of the Edain in Tolkien is suggestive of the longevity of the early Biblical patriarchs. Much longer of course is the life of some of the Elves. Galadriel in particular stands out. It is clear that she was among those present early in the history of the First Age, that is, thousands of years before the reader comes upon her, strong and beautiful in Lothlórien. Christ, we are told, was alive when the world began, yet, says John, "I myself have seen him with my own eyes and listened to him speak." (I John 1:1, *The Living Bible*) Is one of Tolkien's intentions in giving us Galadriel to remind us not simply of vast time but even the eternality of Christ?

It is also possible that there is some parallel between the division of the Hebrews, as time went on, into tribes, and the migrations and settlements into small kingdoms of Elves, Dwarves and Men. We are told that the Elves "made all the old words" (II, 85) and the Bible says that "Adam gave names to all cattle, and to the fowl of the air, and to every beast of the field" (Genesis 2:20). Other correspondences are possible.

In this connection I should mention a lengthy account which Tolkien asked me to read. It was in the form of a Job-like conversation on soul and body and the possible purpose of God in allowing the Fall so that He could manifest

His own sovereignty over Satan all the more, of Christ's incarnation, the spread of His light from one person to another, and the final consummation at Christ's return. He said he was not certain whether to include this in *The Silmarillion* or publish it separately.

If I am correct about the extent of this Biblical orientation, we may be able to conclude that the Valar (angels) are still executing the will of Eru and that our earth will not always experience change and decay but have its own final eucatastrophe. And it is possible that Tolkien is also suggesting that Elves, "a race now abandoned to folk-tales" (III, 519), where only a shadow of truth is preserved, but who once had close affiliations with Men, will then arise from their long concealment and live with us again in some Lothlórien. After all, we have been told that Lúthien's line is never to fail.

The tree, so much loved by Tolkien, is a persistent image both in his writings and also in the Bible, particularly as symbol of beginnings and endings, of significant people and of highly historical events. The opening chapters of the Bible present a garden containing the tree of life and it closes with the same tree in the recreated New Jerusalem. In the early history of Middle-earth two trees, Telperion and Laurelin, white and golden, gave glorious light to Valinor (I, 260; II, 423; III, 308-309), and millennia afterwards the flowering of the scion of Telperion in Minas Tirith marked both the victory over Sauron and the restoration of the Kingdom of Gondor under its newly crowned King Elessar. The ancient lineage of that scion is clear. "There in the courts of the King grew a white tree, from the seed of that tree which Isildur brought over the deep waters, and the seed of that tree before came from Eressëa, and before that out of the Uttermost West in the Day before days when the world was young." (I, 321.)

Minas Tirith itself is not unlike the New Jerusalem, both being dominated by the splendor of light. Gandalf took

Aragorn up Mount Mindolluin in the early morning and they looked down and saw "the towers of the City far below them like white pencils touched by the sunlight, and all the vale of Anduin was like a garden, and the Mountains of Shadow were veiled in a golden mist." (III, 307) In next to the last chapter of the Bible an angel came to John and carried him to a high mountain and showed him "that great city, the holy Jerusalem, descending out of heaven from God, having the glory of God. . . . And the city had no need of the sun . . . for the glory of God did lighten it." (Rev. 21:10-11, 23)

Glorious as Minas Tirith appeared below them, and splendid as the victory over Sauron had been, Aragorn reminded Gandalf that he would die and inquired who would be king over Gondor after him. What he wanted was the assurance of something permanent. He reminded Gandalf that below them the scion of Telperion was still withered and barren and he asked him for "a sign that it would ever be otherwise." The history of mankind and the history of Middle-earth are similar—a perfect beginning followed by centuries of struggle between evil and good with occasional triumphs on one side or the other and no sign of the hoped-for ideal.

What Aragorn asked for was a permanent victory over all such as Sauron and a permanent glory such as he saw by the early morning light. The parallel I am trying to draw might be greatly advanced by what followed Aragorn's question, but actually it is not. Gandalf asked Aragorn to turn away from the beauty below and look "where all seems barren and cold." It was there, to Aragorn's surprise, that he saw the sapling in the rocks near the snow. The natural parallel here is Isaiah's prophecy of Christ as "a tender plant. . . . a root out of a dry ground." (Is. 53:2) This seems confirmed by Gandalf's question, "Who shall say how it comes here in the appointed hour?" (III, 309) He adds that the life within the tree may "lie sleeping through many long years." So if our efforts to draw parallels is valid, it would appear logical at this point to suggest that Elessar's kingdom would be as permanent as that predicted for Christ. Tolkien's eucatastrophe would eventuate and all would be well forever after.

Yet we know this to be out of keeping with Tolkien's frequent realistic assurances that the whole of the history of Middle-earth after its "Fall" is mainly one of wars and rumors of wars. There is no evidence to suggest that the Fourth Age of Middle-earth is to be different from the other three.

To explain the seeming discrepancy, the Biblical parallel of the tree with its saplings must be noted. Isaiah speaks of King David as "a shoot. . . . and a branch out of the stock of Jesse" (Is. 11:1) and David was himself in turn to be a shoot from which God would raise up "a righteous Branch" and would be called "The Lord our Righteousness." (Is. 23:6) Jesus spoke of himself as "the root and the offspring of David." (Rev. 22:16) So here we have a succession of scions covering a long period of time and seeming to carry us back to Gandalf's question as to how these mysteriously but surely appear in their appointed times.

Thus I think we may assume King Elessar not as the final and undying ruler of Middle-earth but only as one heroic victor in a seemingly endless conflict. He is a David called up from the barrens of sheepherding to lead the kingdom. But like Elessar, David died. Neither was the real Telperion. They were only saplings—very like but also very unlike.

But Tolkien was too pronounced a believer in Christ as the Sovereign Ruler who was to come to leave the matter thus. There is evidence that, had his story continued to its full and concluding end the ubiquitous evil of such as Morgoth and Sauron would have ceased. He intended a final glorious eventuality similar to the one described in the Book of Revelation with the true Telperion reappearing, the earth remade, the lands lying under the waves lifted up, the Silmàrils recovered, Eärendil returned to earth, the Two Trees rekindled in their original light and life-giving power, and the mountains of the Pelori leveled so that the light should go out over all the earth—yes, and the dead be raised and the original purposes of Eru executed.

V

Tolkien, Lewis and Williams

The Inklings, in which J. R. R. Tolkien, C. S. Lewis and Charles Williams were prominent members, was primarily a friendship. The last thing they anticipated was the forming of a "school." The Inklings as an organization is more our conception after the fact than it ever was a reality. The particular caliber of its members far more than any formal organization justifies us, as we look backward, in our view that a certain sort of history was being made.

I want to discuss the relationships of these three members of the Inklings and to suggest three things about them: 1) their personal relationships, 2) their literary relationships, and 3) what I believe to be the basic elements common to them.

Personal Relationships

Let me take a given year for a vignette of the three, the year 1940, when all were residents of the city of Oxford. In 1940 Lewis was forty-one, Tolkien forty-eight and Williams fifty-four. By then, Lewis and Tolkien were both well known specialists in medieval and renaissance literature at Oxford University. Lewis had published his first book twenty-one years earlier and was the author of eight books. His *Allegory of Love* had given him an international reputation as a medievalist. He had also published two books of poetry, a fictionalized autobiography and a book called *The Problem of Pain*, the last growing out of his conversion to Christianity about 1930.

J. R. R. Tolkien by 1940 had made himself famous as a philologist and authority on Anglo-Saxon and Middle-English. In 1922 he had published *A Middle English Vocabulary* and in 1937 "Beowulf: The Monsters and the Critics," an essay of singular insight. In that same year he had brought out a book of a very different sort. It was called *The Hobbit, or There and Back Again*.

In 1940 Charles Williams, along with his routine labors as an employee of the Oxford University Press, had published twenty-seven books, including volumes of poetry, biography, criticism and six of his seven strange and profound novels.

So when Lewis, Tolkien and Williams gathered together as Inklings in the year 1940 they were by no means amateur writers, having nearly forty books among them, together with many periodical essays, poems, reviews, and the like. Lewis and Tolkien were university men and Williams was soon to be awarded the honorary M.A., because of his brilliant lectures on writers such as Milton, Shakespeare and Dante, and had himself become a university tutor and lecturer.

Actually the Inklings might have met once, twice or not at all in any given week. Or some of them might have gathered in a pub or any other place which suited their liking. Lewis describes the conditions under which Williams read aloud to him and Tolkien the first two chapters of his Arthurian poem on Taliessin. "Picture to yourself," he said, "an upstairs sitting-room with windows looking north in the 'grove' of Magdalen College on a sunshiny Monday morning in vacation at about ten o'clock. The Prof and I, both on the chesterfield, lit our pipes and stretched out our legs. Williams in the arm-chair opposite to us threw his cigarette into the grate, took up a pile of extremely small, loose sheets on which he habitually wrote—they came, I think, from a twopenny pad for memoranda—and began."[28] The really noteworthy thing about this meeting is its pleasure, not its formality.

More usually, the Inklings met on Thursday evenings. Lewis wrote his brother, then in Shanghai, of one gathering when there was read "a section of the new *Hobbit* book from Tolkien, a nativity play from Charles Williams (unusually intelligible for him, and approved by all), and a chapter out of the book on the Problem of Pain from me.[29] Again Lewis wrote his brother of a meeting in which Dr. Havard read a short paper on clinical experience with the effects of pain. It was an evening "almost equally compounded of merriment, piety, and literature." Lewis added that the Inklings is "now really very well provided, with Adam Fox as chaplain, you as army, Barfield as lawyer, Havard as doctor—almost all the estates—except of course anyone who could actually produce a single necessity of life—a loaf, a boot, or a hut."[30] If the beginning of the Inklings is rather obscure the end is not, for the gatherings ceased at Lewis's death in 1963.

Tolkien and Lewis were at least casually acquainted by the middle of the 1920s, being both members of Oxford University. By 1929 they were close friends. Lewis wrote Arthur Greeves late that year that he had been up until 2:30 a.m. talking to Tolkien, "the Anglo-Saxon professor... who came back with me to College from a society and sat discoursing of the gods and giants and Asgard for three hours, then departing in the wind and rain—who could turn him out, for the fire was bright and the talk good." On another occasion it was 4:00 a.m. when Lewis finally got to bed.[31] To his surprise Lewis discovered that Tolkien was descended from Saxon nobility. His forebears had come to England when Frederick the Great captured Saxony and offered the natives the alternatives of submission or exile. The ancestors of Tolkien had chosen the latter. "Tolkien," Lewis wrote, "is the very last of my friends whom I should have suspected of being *geboren*."[32]

In another of their early meetings Tolkien expounded on the home and how the atmosphere of it must have been different "in the days when a family had fed on the produce of the same few miles of country for six generations, and that perhaps this was why they saw nymphs in the fountains and dryads in the wood—they were not mistaken for there was in a sense *real* (not metaphorical) connections between them and the countryside. What had been earth and air and later corn, and later still bread, really was *in* them. We of course who live on a standarized international diet . . . are artificial beings and have no connection (save in sentiment) with any place on earth. We are synthetic men, uprooted. The strength of the hills is not ours."[33] One can imagine the excitement of such a subject between men of their caliber.

By 1931 Tolkien made it a habit to drop in on Lewis on Monday mornings for a drink and talk. "This is one of the pleasantest spots in the week," wrote Lewis.[34] To Greeves he wrote that Tolkien's likes were so similar to their own that he would have fitted perfectly into their boyhood loves. Reading *The Hobbit* had turned out "uncanny" because it was "so exactly like what we would both have longed to write (or read) in 1916." One reason suggested was that Tolkien "grew up" on William Morris and George MacDonald.[35]

The friendship between Lewis and Tolkien meant not only talking but also walking and swimming together. By 1930 Lewis had moved to The Kilns, the home he was to occupy the rest of his life. Immediately in front of the house was a pond left where clay had been excavated for brick making. Lewis loved this pond and swam in it once or twice a day when the weather allowed. He and Tolkien would paddle a boat out to the middle of the pond, tie it to a snag there, and dive from it into the water.[36] Any close friend of Lewis's in those days was certain to be invited on one of his lengthy walking tours and Tolkien made at least one such excursion. These cordial relations continued up to the time of Lewis's death in 1963. He and Tolkien lived on the same bus line running east from Oxford, Tolkien being about two miles from the center of Oxford and Lewis about four miles.

Tolkien reported that after the coming of Charles Williams to Oxford he spent a great deal of time with him—"I enjoyed his company: he was gay and amusing." He described Williams as "a comet that appeared out of the blue, passed through the little 'provincial' Oxford solar system, and went out again into the unknown."[37] Tolkien addressed to Charles Williams a long humorous poem in rhymed couplets with objections to his obscurity and commendations of his genuineness as man and Christian writer almost equally mixed. He speaks of

> ... *that dark flux of symbol and event,*
> *where fable, faith, and faërie are blent*
> *with half-guessed meanings to some great intent*
> *I cannot grasp.*[38]

The poem sees Williams taking the chair to read, maybe for hours, in the Inklings, and Tolkien adds his sincere wish to be there on such occasions. Charles Williams's letters to his wife are quite constant in their mention of his being with Lewis and Tolkien. "Tolkien has run up to ask me to speak to the naval cadets" or Tolkien had telephoned to suggest that the two of them go to a nursing home to see Lewis during a spell of illness.[39]

Literary Relationships

Although both R. W. Chapman and Nevill Coghill had told Lewis of Charles Williams, it was not until early in

1936 that Lewis read one of Williams's books. He wrote his friend Greeves of the experience: "I have just read what I think a really great book, *The Place of the Lion*. . . . It is based on the Platonic theory of the other world in which the archetypes of all earthly qualities exist; and in the novel . . . these archetypes begin sucking our world back. The lion of strength appears in the world and strength starts going out of the houses and things into him. The archetypal butterfly (enormous) appears and all the butterflies of the world fly back into him. . . . It is not only a most exciting fantasy, but a deeply religious and (unobtrusively) a profoundly learned book. . . . It deserves reading over and over again."[40] It happened that Williams almost at the same time was discovering Lewis, and so there was an exchange of letters.

Lewis and Williams apparently met a time or two thereafter, but it was not until September, 1939 that they got together regularly, the Oxford University Press having removed from London because of the war. Just after his arrival in Oxford Williams wrote his wife, "I have fled to C. S. Lewis's rooms. . . . He is a great tea-drinker at any hour of night or day, and left a tray for me with milk and tea, and an electric kettle at hand." Thereafter they were together as much as their work and their war services would allow.

Lewis saw and promoted Williams's great talents whenever possible. He helped, for instance, to arrange for Williams to speak on John Milton at the university. As a result, other lectures followed, both inside and outside the university, and in due course an honorary degree was conferred on Williams. Lewis described him as "an ugly man with a rather cockney voice. But no one ever thinks of this for five minutes after he has begun speaking. His face becomes almost angelic. Both in public and in private he is of nearly all the men I have met, the one whose address most overflows with *love*. It is simply irresistible."[41]

Lewis tells how he, his brother Warren, Tolkien (Warren Lewis called him "Tollar") and Williams would meet at times in a pub on Broad Street, Oxford, when "our fun is often so fast and furious that the company probably thinks we're talking bawdy when in fact we're very likely talking theology."[42] This triumvirate was to cease on May 15, 1945. At that time Lewis wrote of his grief for "the death of my great friend Charles Williams, my friend of friends, and comforter of all our little set, the most angelic man."[43] Tolkien also felt the loss and wrote Mrs. Williams, "I have grown to admire and love your husband deeply, and I am more grieved than I can express."[44]

Of course this friendship did not mean that they necessarily approved of each other's writings. Tolkien reported that he and Williams never spoke directly to each other about their authorship. Before they became acquainted he had read some of Williams's books, and in the Inklings he heard Williams read parts of *All Hallows Eve, The Figure of Beatrice* and "the Arthurian matter" but believed that Williams's connection with the Inklings was "in fact an astronomical accident that had no effect on his work, and probably no effect on any of the members except Lewis.[45] In an interview with Henry S. Resnick, Tolkien is reported to have said bluntly, "I have read a good many of his books but I don't like them," and in the same conversation seemingly contradicted his remark to Mrs. Williams at the time of her husband's death by saying, "I didn't know Charles Williams very well."[46]

Lewis apparently thought the least of Williams as a dramatist. Of his novels Lewis's adverse criticism is mainly pointed at their obscurity. Otherwise he liked them. He described Williams's *Many Dimensions* as "the very fine working out of the logical consequences of time-travel."[47] Williams wrote his wife that Lewis had a higher opinion than his own of *All Hallows Eve*.[48]

Lewis's main encomium is reserved for some of Williams's literary criticism and especially for his poetry.

Concerning the criticism, one remark is eminently sufficient. "After Blake," wrote Lewis, "Milton criticism is lost in misunderstanding, and the true line is hardly found again until Mr. Charles Williams's preface."[49] Lewis had no particular enthusiasm for Williams's early poetry but believed his later Arthurian poems "produced word music equalled by only two or three in this century and surpassed by none . . . jewelled with internal rhymes," and on the whole evocative of "a perilous world full of ecstasies and terrors, full of things that gleam and dart," a world of "pomp and ritual," of "strong, roaring, and resonant music." Lewis placed Williams as poet, when at his best, in a class with Spenser.[50]

In a broadcast at the time of Williams's death, Lewis summed up his opinion of Williams as a writer. "I think he gave something I had never seen done before. When I first heard of him I realised this was an author unlike any I had ever met before. And when I started reading him this was entirely borne out. . . . What he has, I think, is a very deep and profound understanding of the moment at which a man departs from the ordinary this-worldly life in either direction of this frontier, what he could call Broceliande, the land of shapes through which you pass either to heaven or hell and that is why some people have found that the characters who embody good in his novels are to them almost as disquieting and repellant as the ones that embody evil, because they are both equally characters departing from the ordinary—well, merry middle-earth, as the Middle Ages would have called it. I don't agree at all myself. I think his good characters are a triumph and he shares this with very few authors, because his good characters are more convincing than his bad ones, more real. He knew more about good than about evil."

Lewis was lavish in his enthusiasm for the genius of Tolkien. He felt that his essay "On Fairy-stories" was the best of its kind.[51] He wrote a close friend of having received the first volume of *The Lord of the Rings* and "gluttonously read two chapters instead of saving it all for the weekend. Wouldn't it be wonderful if it really succeeded (In selling, I mean)? It would inaugurate a new age. Dare we hope?"[52] Lewis's review of this first volume began by saying, "This book is lightning from a clear sky." He went on: "Perhaps no book yet written in the world is quite such a radical instance of what its author has elsewhere called 'sub-creation!' The direct debt . . . which every author must owe to the universe, is here deliberately reduced to the minimum. Not content to create his own story, he creates, with an almost insolent prodigality, the whole world in which it is to move, with its own theology, myths, geography, history, palaeography, languages, and orders of being. . . . The names alone are a feast, whether redolent of quiet countryside (Michael Delving, South Farthing), tall and kingly (Boromir, Faramir, Elendil), loathsome like Smeagol who is also Gollum, or frowning in the evil strength of Barad Dûr or Gorgoroth: yet best of all (Lothlórien, Gilthoniel, Galadriel) when they embody that piercing, high, Elvish beauty of which no other prose writer has captured so much. . . . here are beauties which pierce like swords or burn like cold iron; here is a book that will break your heart."[53] Lewis told one of my friends who was visiting him that *The Lord of the Rings* was as long as the Bible and not a word too long.

Lewis regarded *The Hobbit* as more than plot and exciting adventure. He thought the humorous flurry of the early part shifted into what he called epic. "It is as if the battle of Toad Hall had become a serious *heimsohn* and Badger had begun to talk Njal." He recommended this book to his friend Sister Penelope as "a good fairy story by a Christian for a 12-year old."[54]

Surprisingly, Lewis and Tolkien talked of doing a book together, but Lewis felt it was not very likely to be written since "any book in collaboration with that great, but dilatory and unmethodical man . . . is dated I fear to appear on the Greek Calends."[55]

To a correspondent who thought he saw great similarities between the creative writings of Lewis and Tolkien and wondered about mutual influences, Lewis wrote, "I don't think Tolkien influenced me, and I am certain I didn't influence him. That is, I didn't influence *what* he wrote. My continued encouragement, carried to the point of nagging, influenced him very much to write at all with that gravity and at that length. In other words, I acted as a midwife, not as a father. The similarities between his work and mine are due, I think (a) To nature—temperament, (b) To common sources. We are both soaked in Norse mythology, Geo. MacDonald's fairytales, Homer, *Beowulf*, and medieval romance. Also, of course, we are both Christians (he, as R.C.)."[56]

I have as yet found no record of Charles Williams's opinion of Tolkien as writer. Williams's letters often mention Tolkien. "To-morrow I go to Magdalen at 10:45," he wrote, "where Lewis and Tolkien will put on their gowns and take me to the Divinity Schools." There Williams was to deliver his first lecture at Oxford University.[57] Since Williams was a prolific reviewer of books, it probably means simply that there was nothing by Tolkien for him to comment on in the period of Williams's residency in Oxford. How interesting it would be to see what Williams might have said about *The Lord of the Rings*!

Although Tolkien spoke to me warmly of his long and happy association with Lewis, he also sometimes found fault with him. He mentioned that Lewis "borrowed" from him. I pointed out that Lewis had acknowledged the borrowing of the word "Númenor," but Tolkien insisted there were unacknowledged "echoes" in Lewis. In a letter to Jared C. Lobdell, Tolkien mentioned *eldil* as one example, also *Tinidril* as a composite of his *Idril* and *Tinúviel*.[58] A copy of *Perelandra* given by Tolkien to friends contains one of those equivocal notes characteristic of him. On the jacket he has written: "A bottle of sound vintage (?) I hope!"[59] Tolkien wrote me that he found Lewis's *Letters to an American Lady* "deeply interesting and very moving." I have cited earlier in this volume Tolkien's remark that except for Lewis's encouragement *The Lord of the Rings* might never have been published—warm praise indeed.

Williams reviewed some of Lewis's books. Of *The Problem of Pain* he said, "The great pattern of the book is wrought too deeply into Christian dogma and the name of man ... for one to disagree." He found Lewis's *Beyond Personality* to contain some original thoughts and "as new as the Christian Church." Williams's review of *The Screwtape Letters* took the form of a letter from hell. "If many of the wretches read them, we must be prepared for a serious increase in virtue. They give everything away. In explaining our modes of attack, Screwtape has shown men their best defence.... We must certainly discover how these letters got out and we must prevent them from ever being re-read.... You will send someone to see after Lewis?—some very clever fiend?"[60]

There was at least one clear difference of personal taste among these three men. Both Tolkien and Lewis were avid lovers of nature. It is impossible, for instance, to read *The Lord of the Rings* or Lewis's *Perelandra* without noting an enormous sensitivity to the glory of water, wood and sky. On the other hand, Charles Williams had all but an aversion to the world of nature. He was a Londoner by birth and preference and, like Charles Lamb, loved the great city. Perhaps we can also note a difference in Tolkien and Lewis from Williams in respect to a love of Faërie. The first two find no hesitation in writing of dwarves, elves, humanized trees and the like, and their stories often take place in far away, *numinous* places. On the other hand, Williams's characters and situations are commonplace, even though visited by the occult, the magical and the horrible. It is hard to imagine a Hobbit or an Elf slipping into the pages of a Williams story.

The Common Elements

It seems clear that there are two important elements common to these three men, manifest both in their personal lives and in their works. These are a deep-seated Christianity and a vivid imagination.

Imagination, of course, is an element in all creativity, but in our times it is not usual to find a far-flung imagination combined with orthodox Christianity. In Lewis's *Perelandra*, for instance, we have not simply a "science-fiction" voyage to the planet Venus but also a profound metaphor which suggests what may have been the temptation in the Garden of Eden. In *The Lion, the Witch and the Wardrobe* we have both a delightful set of adventures by children in the land of Narnia and also a moving recall of the death and resurrection of Jesus Christ. In Charles Williams's *Descent into Hell* we find not only human and ghostly characters (once a living man and a ghost look through the same window together) but we also see Pauline Anstruther emerging from the haze of worldly social life into the calm clarity of godliness.

It is not necessary to labor this quality in Williams and Lewis. Readers are clearly aware of its existence. Chad Walsh says that in *Perelandra* he "got the taste and the smell of Christian truth. My senses as well as my soul were baptized. It was as though an intellectual abstraction or speculation had become flesh and dwelt in its solid bodily glory among us."[61] Edmund Fuller describes Charles Williams as a "wholly committed writer. He interprets all of natural or familiar life, plus all of its other extraordinary and mysterious dimensions, in terms of Christian theology."[62] Similar comments might be cited at length.

It is the recognition of Tolkien with Lewis and Williams as a Christian writer that may cause a raising of eyebrows.

I have already discussed this matter and endeavored to show that his main works possess not only religious but strongly Christian overtones. To be sure, no real lover of Tolkien's fiction would want it turned into sermons, no matter how cleverly preached. What he, and also Lewis and Williams, have done in all their best things is mythic. They have discovered a dimension as large as life, indeed as large as eternal life. Nevill Coghill described his friend Lewis as having a "hunger for magnitude," a remark equally applicable to Tolkien and Williams.

It is inevitable that any three writers in close friendship who have read their works to each other, and read them open to criticism and suggestions for improvement, should have an influence on each other. What that influence amounted to is quite another matter. Lewis several times warned that the more specific the claim the more likely it was to be wrong. Our intention here has been simply to identify the nature of the friendship.

A bookseller told me of asking a college girl just why she liked *The Lord of the Rings*. She replied that she liked the story because it had black and white meanings. (Oddly, this is the element which is adversely criticized by Edmund Wilson and certain others.) Certainly it is strange that a story of Elves, orcs and talking trees and of no uncertain moral conduct should have become one of the popular books of our time. When this bookseller asked me for an explanation of such a phenomenon, I said I thought our present world had been so drained of elemental qualities such as the numinous, the supernatural and the wonderful that it had been consequently drained of much—perhaps most—of its natural and religious meaning. Someone wrote me of a sixth-grade pupil who, after reading *The Lord of the Rings*, had cried for two days. I think it must have been a cry for life and meaning and joy from the wasteland which had somehow already managed to capture this boy.

VI

Postscript

John Ronald Reuel Tolkien is dead. He had the life of a mortal man, a little more than threescore years and ten. Yet he had Elvish immortality too, as thousands know from acquiring a measure of it themselves through his works. Tolkien was "otherworldly" in the best sense of that term. Since the news media are overwhelmingly concerned with worldly things, his death received little front-page attention. It is a sign of our sad estate that the most meaningful things are the ones we pay the least public attention to. But those who loved Tolkien knew the true value of the good life, not its mere titillations.

Whether Tolkien will survive as a significant literary figure is a question no man can presently answer. What many of us know now with great assurance is that he survives deeply and joyously in us. A college student wrote, "*The Lord of the Rings* was and will probably be the most significant book of my life." A physician said that the highlight of his four years in medical college was reading Tolkien in his senior year. Another suggested that Tolkien's words say more than words can really say. Still, we cannot prophesy how other generations will receive him.

After Glen GoodKnight telephoned me from California of Tolkien's death, I picked up *The Return of the King* and read of Théoden's funeral rites. As the Riders of the King's House rode about the barrow they sang of the king's renown, and I thought some of their words appropriate to Tolkien himself:

> *Out of doubt, out of dark, to the day's rising*
> *he rode singing into the sun, sword unsheathing.*
> *Hope rekindled, and in hope ended;*
> *over death, over dread, over doom lifted*
> *out of loss, out of life, unto long glory.*

After the burial and the weeping of the women and Théoden left alone in his barrow, the folk gathered to put away sorrow in a great feast in the Golden Hall of the palace. We who loved Tolkien now bear our period of sorrow, but it is tempered already with the joy of knowing that Tolkien's words outlive him, not only in the pages of a book but in our flesh and spirit.

I read also the tale of Aragorn and Arwen and I recalled, as I came to Aragorn's last words before his death, that some of them are also appropriate to their creator. Aragorn told his beloved wife, "Behold! we are not bound for ever to the circles of the world, and beyond them is more than memory." My experience with Tolkien made it clear to me that he was a devout Christian and very sure of a larger fulfillment beyond the grave. So there is reason for us to rejoice in his double immortality both as a Christian believer and as the creator of Hobbits and Elves and Dwarves and Ents, of true beauty and proper terror, of golden localities such as Rivendell and Lothlórien, of a good that properly triumphs and an evil that falls, and of a depth of experience appropriate to a need that cries out in us from the roots of our being.

Notes

[1] His obituary mentions him as " 'the best and worst talker in Oxford'—worst for the rapidity and indistinctness of his speech, and best for the penetration, learning, humour and 'race' of what he said." *Times Literary Supplement*, September 3, 1973. His British secretary told me that she herself failed to understand everything he said. He often added to the difficulty by clamping his pipe between his teeth as he talked. One friend reported him "completely unintelligible" as a speaker.

[2] *The New Yorker*, January 15, 1966.

[3] Unpublished letter to Roger Verhulst, March 9, 1966.

[4] Michael Tolkien, "J. R. R. Tolkien—the Wizard Father," London *Sunday Telegraph* September 9, 1973; J. R. R. Tolkien, London *Daily Telegraph*, July 4, 1972.

[5] *Attacks of Taste*, Ed. Evelyn B. Byrne and Otto M. Penzler, Gotham Book Mart, New York, 1971, p. 43.

[6] I was invited to dinner with some of the faculty at Christ Church and afterwards one member asked me if *The Silmarillion* had any sex, in the modern sense, in it. Next day I mentioned this to Tolkien and, to my surprise, he said he had written a couple of sex stories, though he did not volunteer to show them to me. Readers of *The Lord of the Rings* know of the moving account of love between Arwen and Aragorn, and when *The Silmarillion* is published we shall have others of the same sort, but they are vastly different from what we call sex stories today.

[7] "The Man Who Understands Hobbits," Charlotte and Denis Plimmer, London *Daily Telegraph Magazine*, March 22, 1968.

[8] *Mythprint*, September, 1973.

[9] *Letters of C. S. Lewis*, Edited by W. H. Lewis, Geoffrey Bles Ltd., London, 1966, p. 287.

[10] Unpublished letter to Caroline W. Everett, in her master's thesis, "The Imaginative Fiction of J. R. R. Tolkien."

[11] *Diplomat*, October, 1966, p. 39.

[12] See page 17.

[13] Both these letters to Greeves are unpublished. Lewis adds to the second letter: "Whether it is really *good* (I think it is until the end) is of course another question: still more, whether it will succeed with modern children."

[14] *Letters of C. S. Lewis*, pp. 14, 273; *Of Other Worlds*, p. 49, etc.

[15] Both letters are unpublished. The second one is to Thomas T. Howard and is dated October 28, 1958.

[16] "The Man Who Understands Hobbits," Charlotte and Denis Plimmer, London *Daily Telegraph Magazine*, March 22, 1968.

[17] *Niekas*, 18:43.

[18] "The Man Who Understands Hobbits," *op cit.*

[19]*Letters of C. S. Lewis*, p. 197.

[20]*Tree and Leaf*, pp. 49, 60-61. Compare C. S. Lewis's "Myth Became Fact," in *God in the Dock*, Wm. B. Eerdmans Publishing Company, Grand Rapids, 1970, pp. 63-67.

[21]*The Road Goes Ever On*, p. 65.

[22]*Of Other Worlds*, Geoffrey Bles Ltd., London, 1966, p. 33.

[23]Letter to Father Robert Murray, SJ, quoted by him in *The Tablet*, Sept. 15, 1973.

[24]Translation of Albert S. Cook, Ginn and Company, Boston, 1900.

[25]*Myth, Allegory and Gospel*, Ed. John Warwick Montgomery, Bethany Fellowship Press, Minneapolis, 1974.

[26]"The Quest Hero," *Tolkien and His Critics*, p. 53; *Books with Men Behind Them*, p. 184; "Tolkien's Intentions in *The Lord of the Rings*," Mankato State College Studies in English, p. 18.

[27]Facing the Balrog in their close combat at the end of the journey through Moria, Gandalf said, "I am a servant of the Secret Fire." (I, 429)

[28]*Arthurian Torso*, pp. 1-2.

[29]*Letters of C. S. Lewis*, p. 170. The "new *Hobbit*" was of course *The Lord of the Rings* and the nativity play was *Seed of Adam*.

[30]*Letters of C. S. Lewis*, p. 176.

[31]Unpublished letters to Arthur Greeves, December 3, 1929 and September 22, 1931.

[32]Unpublished letter to W. H. Lewis, September 10, 1939.

[33]Unpublished letter to Arthur Greeves, June 22, 1930.

[34]*Letters of C. S. Lewis*, p. 145.

[35]Unpublished letter to Authur Greeves, February 4, 1933.

[36]Unpublished letter to Arthur Greeves, June 26, 1930.

[37]Unpublished letter to Roger Verhulst, March 9, 1966.

[38]A copy of this unpublished poem is among Charles William's papers in the Marion E. Wade collection. The whereabouts of the original is not known.

[39]Unpublished letters of January 14, 1944 and July 12, 1944.

[40]Unpublished letter of February 26, 1936.

[41]Letters of C. S. Lewis, pp. 196-197.

[42]Unpublished letter to Arthur Greeves, January 11, 1944.

[43]*Letters of C. S. Lewis*, p. 206.

[44]Unpublished letter of May 15, 1945.

[45]Unpublished letter to Roger Verhulst, March 9, 1966.

[46]*Niekas*, 18:43.

[47]*Letters of C. S. Lewis*, pp. 162-163; *Of Other Worlds*, p. 69.

[48]Unpublished letter of February 28, 1944.

[49]*A Preface to Paradise Lost*, p. 129. The same idea also occurs in Lewis's [9][11]dedication of this work.

[50]*Arthurian Torso*, pp. 192ff; *English Literature in the Sixteenth Century*, p. 372.

[51]*Of Other Worlds*, p. 26.

[52]Unpublished letter to Mrs. Austin Farrer, December 4, 1953.

[53]*Time and Tide*, August, 1954, p. 1082.

[54]*Of Other Worlds*, p. 19; unpublished letter of August 24, 1939.

[55]*Letters of C. S. Lewis*, p. 287.

[56]To Professor Francis Anderson, September 23, 1963. Used by kind permission of its present owner, Robert H. Baylis.

[57]Unpublished letter to his wife, January 29, 1940.

[58]Unpublished letter of July 31, 1964. It is interesting to note an unexpected source apparently used by both Lewis and Tolkien, i.e., place-names from the Fertile Crescent (now the region of Turkey and the lands south and east of it) such as "Arslan-Tash" and also "Warka-Uruk-Erech," "Lagash," and "Uzun."

[59]This volume is in the Marion E. Wade Collection at Wheaton College.

[60]*Theology*, January, 1941; *Time and Tide*, June 16, 1945; *Ibid.*, March 21, 1942.

[61]*Light on C. S. Lewis*, p. 107.

[62]*Books with Men Behind Them*, p. 203.

Index

Other ASLAN Books include

Beyond Science
Denis Alexander

Doubt
Faith in two minds
Os Guinness

East Wind
A story of endurance
and faith in Stalin's death camps.
Maria Linke and Ruth Hunt

The Immigrant
Stories of an exile
Lawrence Dorr

Lord of the Air
Leary, Maharishi, Sai Baba, Jesus. . .
The personal account of a spiritual search
Tal Brooke

Love Reaches Out
Meditations for people in love
Ulrich Schaffer

Mahalia
The authorized biography
of Gospel singer Mahalia Jackson
Laurraine Goreau

Tomorrow's Television
An examination of British broadcasting past,
present and future
Andrew Quicke